Not<small>ON</small>
<small>MY</small>Watch

A Leader's Guide to Navigate the Impending
Retirement Bubble Disaster, Build a Strong Bench
and Leave a Legacy of Success

Stephen Xavier
America's Top Coach®

ISBN: 1-4392-6185-7

Cover design and illustration by Alvalyn Lundgren
Interior page design and typography by Alvalyn Lundgren, Alvalyn Creative

DEDICATION

I truly believe there is no higher or more noble purpose in this life for a man than to guide, direct, love and cherish his children. With that, I dedicate this book to my two beautiful, shining lights, Isabella and Evan.

ACKNOWLEDGMENTS

First and foremost, I want to thank Ken LaCorte, VP Fox News, for drinks at the Four Seasons Hotel Westlake Village, California. His motivational tirade took me from "wanting to publish my book right" to "getting the freaking thing published!" Thanks, Ken. Thanks also to Cindy Rakowitz for moderating your two "right-wing buddies."

Next, I want to thank Alice Shepherd and Gerri Knilans at Trade Press Services for their expert guidance, support, nagging, and exceptional editorial support and skill. This book would not have happened without you two. Of that, I have no doubt. And, to Alvalyn Lundgren of Alvalyn Creative for your expert design services on this book and everything Cornerstone. Thank you for your wonderful design work and aesthetic sense. Your creative services are highly valued here.

To my clients—although I cannot name names so that I may "protect the innocent" (and others as well!)—from Amgen, BMW, Disney, ABC Television, Glaxo, Goldman, Sachs & Co., Southern California Edison, Edison Mission Energy, Xerox and others too numerous to mention; you are wonderful leaders and without all of you, there would have been no content to write this book. My exposure to you created the laboratory in which I was able, and so fortunate, to practice my craft, support our mutual growth, and teach and learn as well. Thank you. You know who you are. I am grateful to you all.

To my staff and associates at Cornerstone Executive Development Group—your amazing support, skills and professionalism and dedication to making us the best speaks volumes about who you are as people and professionals. How fortunate I am to have all of you to support me and that your faith in me as your "fearless leader" continues.

To my family—Mia, Isabella, Evan, and Boo—you create a space for me called home and for that place, and all of you, I am truly grateful. Yes, I can be difficult at times to live with ☺, but hey, who isn't? We just keep chugging along with faith and love.

To my parents Ed and Barbara—to say I wouldn't have made it this far without your support would be an understatement. Your encouragement on every level for so many years is a selfless act of kindness and I have no words to even begin to express my gratitude. Thank you for your endless love, support, and generosity.

To John Barron, who has quietly worked with me behind the scenes to keep me happy, healthy, and whole for what seems like an eternity (in a good way, of course). Your compassion, kindness, thoughtfulness, and skill have taught me so much on so many levels. There are no words to express the impact you have had on my life, both personally and professionally. I believe you have been the glue that has kept me together. Thank you.

And last, but surely not least, to the BR Public Relations team—Cindy Rakowitz, Diane Black, Jan Andrews and staff—we could not find four more unlikely people (you three and myself) to throw together as a team! Your love and support, professionalism and commitment to "put me on the map" were nothing less than extraordinary. Thank you for your service, your partnering, and your constant nagging. It all worked!

CONTENTS

AN URGENT CALL TO ACTION

This book is for the legions of leaders, managers, and executives—corporate and otherwise—who have done little so far to create a space where the "tribal knowledge" of their office or organization can be passed along to the next generation of emerging leaders. Doing something about that right now is extremely critical because the Baby Boomer retirement bubble is about to burst. It has actually already begun, but this current economic crisis has slowed it down – temporarily.

For over ten years, AARP and the Society for Human Resource Management (SHRM) have been sounding alarms about the Baby Boomer retirement bubble, predicting serious leadership vacuums and productivity shortfalls that could undermine the nation's global competitiveness. Even though the current economic plight has bought industry an additional year or so to address the looming workforce and management talent shortage, the dire warnings will still come true, just a little later than originally anticipated. If current leaders do not take advantage of this last-minute reprieve to build bench strength now, they will not get a second chance. Without immediate action, organizations devastated by economic setbacks will face another disaster— *a brain drain never before seen in the history of this country.*

Already, a lack of leadership is hindering performance at more than half (56 percent) of the 1,100 organizations polled in Aon Consulting's 2008 Benefits and Talent Survey as cited by *Human Resource Executive Online* ("A Leadership Shortage" by Anne Freedman, December 1, 2008). In addition, 31 percent expected their performance to be impacted by a shortage of leaders in the next one to four years.

The business emphasis on day-to-day operations and short-term financial results usually has leaders focused on the here and now, keeping them too busy to pay attention to who will soon fill their shoes. "Most companies maintain their office copiers better than they build the capabilities of their people, especially the ones who are supposed to be future leaders," says American Express chief Ken Chenault, "and for decades they've gotten away with it." according to the Fortune magazine article, "How top companies breed stars" by Geoff Colvin, September 2007. Now, "companies that were never especially serious about leadership development are getting serious... The world's best companies realize that no matter what business they're in, their real business is building leaders."

When senior leaders depart—either suddenly or for long-expected retirement—organizations that have not developed emerging talent are left "upside-down" with no "bench" from which to draw qualified replacement talent. Consider this analogy: Senior leaders are the best players actively engaged on the ball court. Meanwhile, waiting on that bench should also be well-trained, well-coached substitutes who can be called upon to step in at a moment's notice. In business, these well-prepared substitute players are needed to maintain the continuity of leadership so that companies can stay viable from generation to generation.

There is yet another critical need that well-prepared new players can fulfill. They can lighten the burden of weary leaders. Today's executives are experiencing a new kind of vulnerability that didn't exist twenty years ago. They are running as fast as they can, and yet, it never seems fast enough. They still struggle to keep themselves, their people, and their companies ahead of the curve in the nonstop treadmill of the ever-changing global economy—all the while dealing with the unrelenting demand for immediate gratification from boards and shareholders, uncompromising expectations of superior quality from customers, constantly evolving technologies, 24/7 communication capabilities, and the need for extraordinary business agility. Add to these external factors the emotionally draining challenges presented by an evolving workforce and the coming avalanche of Baby Boomer retirement, and the race seems truly overwhelming. So, the question is: how can leaders possibly stay on top of it all and, at the same time, keep their companies viable? The answers lie not in more sophisticated business models. These only add to the daunting complexity that challenges leaders to the limit. And let's face facts: since the end of the twentieth century, how many "business development" or "business improvement" models have actually been successful? The answer: very few or maybe even none. Rather, the true solution to catching up and staying ahead lies in simplicity. The simple solution is for executives to develop emerging talent around them now—talent that will lighten their load while creating bench strength for the near- and long-term future of the organization.

Why should it be the job of current leaders, who have too much on their plates as it is, to develop their successors? Unfortunately, they have no choice because the two traditional approaches to developing new leadership have proven to be only marginally successful at best. The first is the B-school model, which produces graduates chock-full of theory, but devoid of practical knowledge. Experience has taught us that extensive multifaceted, sophisticated training in the form of executive programs at universities often fail to deliver the expected results. Young executives return with certificates, no better off than they were tens of thousands of dollars ago. Besides, those same institutions of higher learning have given us much bad advice in the form of brainchildren like rightsizing, downsizing, and reengineering, all of which have proven to be abysmal failures in real-world application. Millions of business bestsellers outlining these "successful processes" were sold. Reviewers raved about them, and their authors charged exorbitant speaking fees. Yet, in actual practice, the directed change was, in most cases, neither lasting nor beneficial to the recipient. Only the consultants who designed and delivered the programs profited from this one-size-fits-all approach. It's no wonder that Bernard Baruch's old adage, "If all you have is a hammer, everything looks like a nail" has dogged consultants for decades! And as for the leaders who attempted to force their organizations into these models, they have found themselves leading change efforts that were good in theory but devoid of measurable, sustainable results. One cannot lead or develop people this way. It's like the infamous shell game, with no winners, only losers.

The second time-honored method of preparing future leaders is the "seat-of-your-pants" approach to executive development. People proceed through their entire careers, learning as they go, typically without any focus or structure to their advancement. Through sheer serendipity, a substantial percentage of people manage to learn from experience and go on to become decent managers or leaders. But a greater number are not so fortunate. They make the same mistakes repeatedly or continue to rely on a few strengths that served them in the past. This approach may get them ahead in the short- term, but in the long-term, it's unsustainable. Eventually, over-reliance on those few strengths causes executives to derail as their responsibilities broaden and their number of direct reports increases.

Despite investments in MBA and certificate programs at "Ivy League" schools, more and more companies, regardless of size and industry, are beginning to realize that what their emerging talent needs is "boot camp"—or Management 101 or Leadership 101, so to speak. Surprisingly, young executives lack very basic skills. As a matter of fact, and even more astonishingly, many senior executives fare poorly in those same fundamental skills as well—planning, delegating, communicating, coaching, training, and giving feedback. As a result, they cannot create an environment that engenders trust and accountability, which in turn hinders their protégés' ability to take significant leaps forward.

Further, in the absence of these very basic skills and without a strategic, methodical approach to career development, leaders usually fall victim to a promotion dynamic I call the "enchantment factor." It refers to a tendency to promote young executives based on their ability to "manage up" effectively or based on isolated project successes. Through a polished executive presence and superb presentation skills, up-and-coming go-getters cast a spell on senior leaders that leaves them blind to any potential weaknesses. Then, soon after the promotion, the Peter Principle rears its ugly head. Named after author Dr. Laurence J. Peter, it holds that "in a hierarchy, every employee tends to rise to his level of incompetence." Suddenly, the new executive's responsibilities have grown with a considerably higher number of direct reports, and now, the individual is scrambling to catch up to a level for which he or she was woefully unprepared. In the strategic approach to targeted development advocated here, objective assessment and observation across multiple projects over time actually prevent the promotion of emerging talent based on isolated project successes or magic spells.

The problem of leadership succession is as old as leadership itself. But the leadership vacuum that will be created when the Baby Boomer retirement bubble bursts will be like none before in history. It cannot be filled using the traditional approaches to executive succession—like the B-school model, the seat-of-your-pants model, picking and grooming a well-liked individual, opting for the "obvious choice," or selecting someone who has "paid their dues."

But there is a new model, and it works. Its basis is simple: Pick the best and the brightest, identify their growth needs, invest effort and resources in developing the most promising talent individually and, most importantly, cultivate several individuals together as a future leadership team. And finally, do it now!

The development of future leaders is not the job of the Human Resource department. Rather, the task falls on the shoulders of the only people who are truly qualified to handle it—current leadership. "HR is the corporate function with the greatest potential—the key driver, in theory, of business performance—and also the one that most consistently under-delivers," observed Keith H. Hammonds in "Why We Hate HR," a *Fast Company* article, December 19, 2007. "After close to 20 years of hopeful rhetoric about becoming 'strategic partners' with a 'seat at the table' where the business decisions that matter are made, most human-resources professionals aren't nearly there." Part of the evidence is that, according to SHRM's own studies, only a one-quarter of HR professionals are convinced that the flood of retiring Baby Boomers would be a problem for their organization—despite a 2005 warning from SHRM President Susan R. Meisinger that the evolving demographic changes present major challenges to America's workplace.

Although some HR departments have paid attention to the warnings, their response has been woefully inadequate. They created succession, or rather replacement plans, but only in a check-off-the-box fashion. They did not take the trouble to assess the actual leadership skills of proposed succession candidates and did nothing to develop them towards a future career path.

Although driven by the need to reach corporate goals, including bottom line results, leaders also have a responsibility to plan for succession and create bench strength for the future success of the organization. No one is better qualified to develop a company's future leaders than its current leaders.

How to Use This Book

This book contains practical solutions executives can apply now to impart fundamental leadership skills to emerging talent. Unlike most books on this topic, this is a hands-on owner's manual with simple, proven tools and advice that executives can use right now to identify top talent in their organizations, foster the development of high-potential talent and create the legacy of leadership that is so sorely needed in American enterprise (and elsewhere) today.

The methods and approaches in this book are not gimmicks. They are time-tested and have been utilized by myself and the coaches of my company, Cornerstone Executive Development Group, with hundreds of our clients and their leaders. They were developed in real organizations and with real people to solve real problems. However, while these tools have been utilized in a wide range of organizations and industries, they are not cookie-cutter answers, but rather solutions that transcend any particular enterprise or industry. What they lack in theory, they more than compensate for in real results.

Although each chapter stands on its own and can be used to achieve immediate value, readers will gain the most benefit from reading all chapters and applying the entire process to prepare well-rounded future leaders.

Each chapter includes:

- Concrete steps for a focused strategic approach to leadership development;
- Case studies that demonstrate real-world application;
- Exercises to practice new skills; and
- References to additional materials of interest.

Here is a brief overview of the chapters to come:

Chapter One: *Coaching for Success*

Coaching is one of the most powerful means of developing the next generation of leaders and, at the same time, building strong executive teams for the present and future. This chapter outlines a simple process anyone in a management or leadership position can use to become a coach to emerging talent. Readers who follow the steps shown here—consistently with competence and compassion—will soon see measurable, constructive change in their people and organization. As they establish coaching relationships, they will improve communication and foster mutual trust and support. They will bring out the genius in each employee and create a "success environment," where people operate with greater efficiency, higher productivity, and more enthusiasm. Ultimately, they will create the bench strength to meet current and future business needs.

Chapter Two: *Feedback —The Breakfast of Champions*

Feedback is designed to deliver information about performance in a way that is non-judgmental and non-defensive. The coach gives praise for jobs well done and tasks that have been accomplished. In addition, the coach provides the coachee with meaningful direction when needed to reset course. This chapter outlines the seven-step feedback model executives will use to share data with their coachees. Leaders will learn how to use feedback in coaching their highest performers, as well as how to use feedback for performance management, i.e., coaching low or marginal performers—either toward success—or toward the door. Executives will learn how to determine a coachee's skill level and coaching needs, and how to use the right types and amount of feedback consistently and competently to move coachees toward action and improvement.

Chapter Three: *Making Communication Work*

Because leaders find themselves doing a great deal of talking, they often think they are good communicators. But good communications are a matter of quality, not quantity. Unless executives can articulately and intelligently relate to and communicate with people all around them, even the greatest ideas will never materialize. In order to coach people effectively, motivate and influence others, build relationships and resolve conflict, executives need superb verbal, non-verbal, and listening skills to be truly good communicators. In this chapter, executives will learn the simple basics of good communication skills so they can execute strategy, give direction on roles and responsibilities, and coach emerging talent. They will learn how to identify the right communication style appropriate to a specific audience; how to plan a clear, concise presentation; how to give feedback to coachees on the effectiveness of their communication; and how to practice communication skills and model them for emerging leaders.

Chapter Four: *The Art of Managing Conflict*

Without steadfast conflict management skills, many executives avoid conflict altogether. This leaves loose ends and undermines relationships because issues are left unresolved. Unmanaged conflict usually turns into third-party chatter, which fuels many of the fires leaders are so busy putting out. The results are poor morale and unproductive people. To use another analogy, unmanaged conflict is like running a race with shoelaces tied to each other — it's always a snag, limiting action and eventually tripping up executives as they attempt to leap ahead in the race for success. This chapter shows leaders practical tools to develop mature conflict management skills for themselves and within their teams so that issues can be addressed in real time — before they escalate. Leaders will learn how to create clarity around differences in viewpoints, balance different approaches to problem solving and put disagreement among individuals to productive use.

Chapter Five: *Building Relationships — For Real*

People in the up-and-comer ranks often focus on competing with their peers rather than with competitors in their industry—the true competition. Then, as they advance in the organization, they eventually become peers at a senior executive level where they need to be teammates rather than opponents. That's why building peer relationships is a critical skill at any level. Yes, most senior executives neglect seeing high-potential people in the lower ranks as part of a future leadership team. In this chapter, they will learn how to coach their team members to develop and nurture relationships with peers, direct reports, bosses, and other stakeholders. They will become skilled at coaching emerging talent to cooperate and collaborate rather than compete with their peers. Since true success is built on a foundation of accomplishments of the people below, emerging leaders will also discover how to build positive relationships with their direct reports to create undying loyalty and trust.

Chapter Six: *Mastering the Art of Motivation*

Contrary to popular belief, motivating employees is rarely a matter of enticing them with financial incentives. Research has shown that pay raises, plush offices, perks, and promotions drive people to perform only as long as it takes to get the next raise or promotion. True motivation, on the other hand, comes from intrinsic factors that answer people's deep-seated need for growth and achievement. In this chapter, executives will learn how to measure their people's current level of motivation, what really motivates people, and how to apply simple tools to become more proactive and consistent in keeping their people highly energized and enthusiastic. They will learn how to create an environment where morale is high and employees work more efficiently and productively. They will also learn how to transfer their new motivating skills to direct reports so they, in turn, can better motivate their team members.

Chapter Seven: *Harnessing the Power of Influence*

Influence is defined as the action or process of producing effects on others by intangible or indirect means. Since the pursuit of leadership basically amounts to getting things done through others, what could be more critical in a leadership position than being an excellent influencer? Contrary to its negative stigma, influencing is not about manipulating others through overt or covert means. Rather, it's a powerful, constructive leadership tool that furthers rapport, trust, and cooperation for the purpose of garnering resources and support. This chapter shows leaders the many areas where they can increase their efficiency and effectiveness by becoming better influencers. Through a simple four-step process, they will develop better influencing skills and learn how to transfer those skills to the emerging generation of leaders.

Chapter Eight: *Strategic Thinking Makes the Leader*

In order to rise to a senior leadership position, junior executives and managers need to develop a broader sense of vision—the "big picture" thinking that distinguishes leadership from management. Particularly, emerging talent with a science, engineering, accounting, or similar technical background is often held back by a narrow focus on the work at hand. In this chapter, leaders will learn specific steps they can take to turn junior executives into strategic thinkers, and teach them the art and science of strategic planning.

Through exercises and feedback, emerging leaders will expand their peripheral vision, think more creatively, and plan in accordance with a strategic vision.

Chapter Nine: *Real Diversity for the New Millennium*

Diversity is not just about gender and race, but also about cultural and socioeconomic background, education, skill sets, and even personality. One successful leader had a very unusual rule when it came to external recruiting and hiring: he would always hire the candidate everyone liked the least. He did this because that individual could be counted upon to be different, and thus, contribute something fresh to the team's perspective. Not every executive may have the courage to go to such an extreme, but the creation and management of a diverse workforce should be among the priorities for any organization. This chapter suggests some simple actions that leaders can take to enhance and encourage diversity in their organizations, and coach junior executives to manage the unique challenges that come with creating and managing a diverse workforce.

Chapter Ten: *Change Management: Developing a Flexible, High-Trust Culture*

Sometimes even successful teams get stuck in a rut and follow the same old formulas year after year. Although the formula may be successful to a point, eventually it will cause them to derail as the internal or external environment changes. Fortunately, flexibility and managing change are skills that can be taught. This chapter provides steps leaders can take to utilize instinct and emotional intelligence to become more flexible and adaptable, both in responding to environmental changes and in initiating change to leap ahead of the competition. Executives will also learn how to coach emerging talent in the essential skills of agility and flexibility. Rather than feeling insecure about the unknowns of tomorrow, executives will learn to maintain high morale and adaptability to meet the ever-changing needs of the global economy.

Chapter Eleven: *How to Identify Competent Talent:*
A Checklist for Leaders

In the process of coaching or preparing to coach an organization's emerging talent, leaders may wonder how to identify the best candidates for coaching. Who among all those promising young managers and executives has the best chance of one day rising to a senior leadership position or even filling the leader's shoes? Further, candidates previously considered marginal by the leader may begin to blossom in the process of coaching and emerge as very high-potential leadership talent. This chapter provides the do's and don'ts for identifying hidden talent so that the best possible candidates can be coached and developed for maximum benefit to the coachee, the leader, and the organization.

Appendix: Assessments —
Setting the Stage for Development

In order to effectively assess your employees' strengths and weaknesses in preparation for executive development and coaching, it's necessary to gather performance data in an objective and somewhat dispassionate way. Since most of us have blind spots about ourselves, we cannot be counted on to give an unbiased appraisal of our own strengths and weaknesses, nor can we serve as the only source of an objective evaluation of those around us. Accordingly, the best place to start assessing emerging leaders and other possible high-potential candidates is by using a 360 Degree Feedback instrument. A 360 assessment is a snapshot in time in that it measures behaviors and performance, which can change, rather than innate personality traits, which remain fairly static. It's a tool that gathers feedback from people all around the coachee and across the organization—superiors, peers, colleagues, and direct and indirect reports. This section provides an understanding about the basics of assessment. In some cases, executives may wish to work with their human resources department in developing and implementing the assessment process.

CHAPTER ONE
COACHING FOR SUCCESS

It would be better if you began to teach others only
after you yourself have learned something.
— Albert Einstein

Executive coaching is a well-known business term, but few people really understand what it is or why it's important. The reality is: executive coaching is one of the most powerful means of developing emerging leaders and, at the same time, building strong executive teams for the present and future. Executive coaches help individuals:

➤ Break through personal and organizational barriers so they can achieve peak performance, especially during periods of change

➤ Perform exceptionally in current roles

➤ Become prepared for future roles

➤ Learn constructive ways of resolving conflict between individuals, within teams, and across departments

➤ Recognize and eliminate the barriers that interfere with creativity, productivity, and goal attainment

➤ Stimulate self-directed career development and engage in development with the support of internal, senior executives who are champions-as-mentors

And, who better to coach emerging talent to become the next generation of leaders than experienced senior executives? They are uniquely positioned to serve as role models because they understand what it takes to become and remain successful in an extremely competitive and ever-changing business climate. When they have substantial tenure with the company, they also have in-depth knowledge of its organizational systems and cultures, and how those two factors influence individual performance and the selection of future leaders.

This chapter outlines a simple process leaders can use to become coaches to emerging talent. Leaders who follow the steps shown here with consistency, competency, and compassion, will soon see significant, measurable constructive change in their people and organization. When coaching relationships are established, they will improve communication and foster mutual trust and support. Through this process, leaders will bring out the genius in each employee and create a success environment, where people can operate with greater efficiency, higher productivity, and more enthusiasm. Ultimately, this process enables leaders to create the bench strength necessary to meet future business needs while fulfilling the current needs of the organization and its customers.

Coaching: What It Is and Isn't

One fundamental principle of good coaching is to recognize and understand that it's not designed to fundamentally or solely change the individual being coached. Rather, it's to illuminate the individual and organizational dynamics that may detract the emerging leader from achieving peak performance. At the same time, the purpose is to help coachees develop specific alternative behaviors and success performance levels that are missing from their current repertoire of skills. In turn, coachees can then exercise influence around them and bring about positive organizational change.

Coaching is not a technique, but a professional, confidential, and honest relationship between a coach and coachee—whether the coach is internal or external. It enables both parties to explore barriers to overcome and identify strengths upon which to build. The desired outcome is sustained peak performance and career satisfaction for the coachee *and* success for the organization.

Coaching vs. Mentoring

Coaching and mentoring, in the purest sense, are about teaching and guiding, respectively. As coaches, leaders teach, as mentors they guide. Both are best done by example, in the form of giving advice and providing insight grounded in broad experience. But coaching and mentoring have different purposes. Coaching is a short-term performance improvement process, while mentoring is long-term career development.

Coaching and mentoring, in the purest sense, are about teaching and guiding, respectively. As coaches, leaders teach, as mentors they guide. Both are best done by example, in the form of giving advice and providing insight grounded in broad experience. But coaching and mentoring have different purposes. Coaching is a short-term performance improvement process, while mentoring is long-term career development.

Unlike coaching, which can be effectively accomplished by either outside consultants or company executives, mentoring is an internal learning process, which only mature organizations can effectively utilize. A mature organization is one that is very flat or, if hierarchical, has wide-open communication channels across all levels. Mature organizations are also very fluid. For example, they support people who want to move across business unit lines, and they encourage employees to cross-train so that everyone understands what everyone else is doing in accomplishing the common goal—serving the customer and adding to the company's overall bottom line. Mentoring requires such a mature organization, stellar communication models and the establishment of a solid infrastructure around assessment.

Coaching should not be confrontational for the purpose of fixing problem behaviors (i.e., "You can't do this!" or "Don't do that!"). The coach typically does not give directions or orders. Nor does a coach provide merely feedback and advice. Rather, he or she equips the coachee with the insight, knowledge, skills and ability to create or take advantage of new opportunities by helping to broaden the coachee's perception.

Present-day leadership development practices often draw a distinction between two types of coaching: performance coaching and developmental coaching. *Performance coaching* clarifies performance expectations, identifies shortfalls, pinpoints a higher level of performance, identifies strategies for achieving the new level of performance, and establishes commitment to continuous improvement towards the defined new level. *Developmental coaching* unlocks the coachee's potential to maximize his or her performance through the facilitation of a coach.

The former method predominates in executive coaching, perhaps due to the powerful demand for management development processes that deliver measurable improvements in performance and business results. In actual practice, however, a combination of the two methods deepens and enriches the process and ensures greater levels of success. Executives who have benefited from this combined approach have been more likely to complete coaching engagements with significant performance improvements. More notably, many become coaches themselves and are able to pass on their newly gained expertise and insights to direct reports.

Here are a few examples of areas most commonly underdeveloped or underutilized in current and emerging leaders that can be addressed in coaching:

➢**Broaden active listening skills:** Good listening skills require someone to listen actively and with empathy, and to leave the speaker left feeling heard and acknowledged.

➢**Improve and enhance overall communication style:** Consciously engage in strategic and dynamic conversations that involve active listening, clarifying, and responding where needed, and articulating one's own thoughts clearly and concisely.

➤**Increase awareness of impact on others:** Strengthen your own "radar" or sensitivity, and get a sense of others' feelings and needs and how your style impacts those around you.

➤**Strategic thinking.** Too often, the strategy of leaders is "ready, fire, aim!" Rather, well-thought-out plans should be the result of thinking creatively, enrolling others in the process to gain a perspective broader than your own, and having a clear plan of execution to make your thinking a reality.

➤**Business acumen:** Learning the most about your own areas of responsibility and then making it your business to learn about others' areas to broaden your own knowledge and strengthen your organizational, managerial, and personal contribution to success.

➤**Building and managing a diverse workforce:** Engage in true diversity—the diversity of attracting and effectively managing people who are truly different from you and your team in how they think, communicate, relate, and problem solve. This approach goes far beyond the typical definition of diversity, which focuses almost solely on race, gender, age, and other personal attributes.

➤**Relationship building:** If you have a few good relationships throughout the organization, build more. If you have many, make them deeper! By the time you need better relationships to get something done, it's already too late to build them.

➤**Focus and follow-through:** As Grandpa used to say, "The road to hell is paved with good intentions." The same could be said of plans. When you make plans, stay focused on the execution, follow through with commitments, and always be ready to re-navigate when needed to reach desired goals.

Finally, it's important to understand coaching is *not* therapy. It's not about changing the person. It's about enhancing abilities or altering specific behaviors that do not work for individuals in their current roles or will not work for them in expanding leadership roles. Coaches identify concrete development areas and help emerging leaders take steps to modify conduct, for example, by being more respectful, sensitive, and more cognizant of the impact they have on others. And although coaching may not be "therapy," do not underestimate the profound impact it can and will have on the coachee. Even under the best of circumstances and with the best candidates, when anyone is "under the microscope" they are going to feel the pressure. Be sensitive to that and coach accordingly.

One rule of thumb: If a coachee is unwilling to recognize his or her own weaknesses and work to overcome them, it's a good sign he or she does not belong in a leadership position. Coaching is a process that can, and does, change the lives of coachees in significant ways. As such, coaches must be aware of the powerful influence they have and wield that power carefully.

Case Study: Using Coaching to Increase Emotional Intelligence

Coaching is an excellent tool to increase an individual's emotional intelligence. Take the case of "Sally" who was a vice president at a global aerospace company. Her boss, "Roger," the senior vice president, had received many complaints about her from colleagues who found her to be unreasonably demanding and, at times, even demeaning. He did not really believe she could change, but agreed to have her coached to develop her emotional intelligence and increase her sensitivity to others.

The first two steps were to conduct a formal assessment to measure Sally's emotional intelligence and a survey of her coworkers. In both cases, Sally's results showed high scores in areas of self-awareness (she was cognizant of her own strengths and weaknesses), but extremely low scores in social awareness (the impact of her behavior on others). When confronted with these findings, she was initially guarded, pointed, and defensive. However, with coaching and practice, her emotional intelligence soon increased to a point where she recognized her interpersonal shortcomings and acknowledged them to all concerned.

With her coach, she worked on creating disciplined behaviors and approaches to dealing more appropriately with her colleagues and also rehearsed new behaviors with the coach. She learned techniques such as breathing slowly, "holding her tongue," counting to five before responding, and how to ask questions to probe for a deeper understanding of a colleague's issue rather than badgering them. None of this came easily. However, almost immediately she received unsolicited, positive feedback on her new approach. The responses from others reinforced the new behaviors and helped others act differently toward her.

Her boss, Roger, on the other hand, provides a good example of what not to do. Although he had agreed to have Sally coached, he had really already given up on her. He had expected her development efforts to fail and had already provided an excuse for firing her. Therefore, no matter how much she changed and how well others responded to her new approach, he continued to find fault. Since Roger was not open to developing his own emotional intelligence, his behavior toward her did not change. Sally eventually decided to leave the company and, due to her newfound higher emotional intelligence, she achieved great success with another employer. Roger remains in his position, and if history is any indicator of future pathways, he is still struggling with "difficult employees" and will continue to do so until his own development becomes a high priority. A quick teaching moment here: as you coach others, realize that you, too, are "being coached." Use the coaching relationship and this opportunity for self-reflection to improve your own self-awareness and develop yourself accordingly.

A lesson to be learned: If you make a commitment to coach and develop an employee and potential successor, do so with the very sincere intention of helping him or her succeed, not as an attempt to "weed them out." The weeding-out approach should occur long before coaching at this level begins, not during or after. Roger's approach shows exactly what not to do.

Three Steps to Coaching

The coaching process typically consists of three steps: 1) planning the coaching engagement, 2) conducting the coaching engagement, and 3) follow-up.

1. *Planning the coaching engagement.*

This phase consists of two steps. The first is to assess the coachee's development needs using a GAPS-style assessment. To facilitate the assessment, you may wish to work with your human resources department to have a 360 Degree Feedback instrument administered on the coachee. However, you need to control the process and data of the assessment, not human resources. There are far too many case studies of overzealous HR staffers who rolled out 360s and then used the data, in one way or another, for an individual's performance review. This is exactly what 360s were not designed for. To misuse this assessment in this way only engenders a loss of trust by employees at-large and further reinforces the view that HR is "the police" and not here to help. The same holds true for you as the executive-as-coach. Your misuse of the data as a "performance measure" can backfire, sending high-potential candidates running for the exits—the exact opposite affect you should want to create. You have been warned! (Refer to the Appendix for further information on assessment.)

A GAPS analysis or assessment for an individual is, in a sense, not unlike the GAPS-style assessment you have very likely used at some time in your career while goal-setting, creating a long-term strategic plan, or assessing current states of projects or organizational performance, etc. That process, tailored here for individual assessment, asks the following questions:

G – Goals: What are the talented individual's short- and long-range career goals? What does he or she need to do in order to reach the next level? What results does he or she need to achieve?

A – Abilities: Which of the individual's existing abilities are the most crucial? What results is he or she already getting? What abilities does he or she need to develop in order to move to the next level? (Please refer to the sidebar of Sample Core Competencies for Emerging Leaders as examples of the abilities a leader may need upon promotion.)

P – Perceptions: What awareness and understanding do emerging leaders have about how their superiors and others see them and what they expect of them? For example: "I see you as needing to develop... because..." or "Your customers want you to... because..." or "You seem most effective at... and the results are..." Here is a key area where 360 data will close any perception gaps the coachee may have.

S – Standards: What standards for development are being set? For example: "In order to truly excel, you will need to develop..." or "The company is looking for... so we can..." or "To move to the next level, you would have to..." Here again, a 360 instrument is an excellent tool with specific data points and suggestions to steer the coachee in the right direction with developmental ideas and tips.

Once the GAPS analysis is complete, the second phase of *planning the coaching engagement* involves goal setting. Make sure individual development goals are closely aligned with departmental and long-term organizational goals. This ensures the individual's growth path is in sync with the direction in which the organization is headed. It also helps keep the coachee on track toward assuming positions of higher responsibility.

To make this part of the planning process effective, use the S.M.A.R.T. acronym in setting goals. Productive goals are:

S – Specific, clear goals; no "fuzzy" or indefinable goals

M–Measurable; goals need to have clear end results that have clear outcomes

A – Agreed upon by coach and coachee

R – Realistic and relevant to the individual's development and the organization's needs

T – Timed; have a set beginning and end timeframe for completion

2. *Conducting the coaching engagement.*

After the assessment is complete and goals have been set, the second phase of the coaching process is the actual implementation of a development plan. Coach and coachee create a coaching partnership. They build rapport, establish trust, and gain agreement on the GAPS identified. I strongly suggest that you use Worksheet 1 printed at the end of this chapter as a guideline for this process.

Discuss the expected benefits of the coaching engagement for the coachee, coach, and the organization. Then agree on the next steps to take and how you will work together—timeframes, frequency of meetings, expectations around what must be achieved during the term of the engagement, etc. You may use Worksheet 2 printed at the end of this chapter to establish the partnership and agreement between coach and coachee and solidly define the next steps.

Work with the coachee on a regular basis for a mutually agreed upon set number of months: three to four-plus hours per month for a period of eight to ten months. Meetings every other week are best; monthly is okay as well but not preferred. Identify two to three behaviors or performance areas that the coachee will work on.

There are coaching models out there that insist "only one development area at a time." In my twenty-plus years of experience I have never seen two to three development areas from a 360 assessment that were not related in some way. There is always a thread that connects them. Look for this thread and what you will find is "layers" of the issues that show up differently but are still related and need to be addressed. Here is an example:

Bill was a highly competent and strong individual contributor. Following his first promotion to a management role, he had a learning curve moving from strong individual contributor to a manager of people, but that is natural for most people. With his next promotion, the number of his direct reports grew from six to sixteen, and that's

A good coach has the courage to say what many think but few will say aloud.

when "the trouble began." Although still liked and respected by peers and direct reports, the rumbling around the water cooler was that he was "caving in" (i.e., spending more time in his office rather than out among his people) and that was a red flag.

When a 360 assessment was conducted, he maintained fairly high scores on performance and delivery as everyone involved had expected; however, when it came to the "care and feeding" of his people, a pattern emerged. On the surface, his number one development area appeared to be: "A Need to Improve Ability to More Effectively Manage Direct Reports," which made sense. However, what followed were the more subtle aspects of development that needed to be acknowledged. His second and third development areas were around a need for improved communication (across all levels) and more effective delegation.

Once you begin to string together the three development areas it's easy to see how they can be simply and inextricably linked. Therefore, they must be viewed and worked on as a "three-pack," and not individually as some experts may suggest.

The delegation piece, for example, may have extended not only to direct reports but also to peers when Bill was leading a cross-functional team. Similarly, his communication skills, I would easily wager, probably fell short not only in a particular area (e.g., direct reports), but likely moved across lines, where it exhibited itself to varying degrees. Nevertheless, it was still an issue that had to be incorporated into the whole development process as a necessary component to round out the candidate.

In designing a coachee's development plan, have him or her identify both strengths that need to be leveraged and the areas of development opportunity that need to be directly addressed. Once these behaviors are identified and validated, have the coachee spell out action items related to each behavior in clear, actionable language. (You may use Worksheet 3 for this purpose, if desired.)

Choose actions that have maximum effectiveness. The most powerful forms of development are on-the-job assignments and special projects. Other forms are formal education and training (e.g., courses, seminars), cross-training, observing experts, practice sessions, videotaping, books, tapes, articles, informal day-to-day tips, and self-study programs. Match assignments to organizational needs such as helping the company successfully complete a critical change initiative, enhance its competitive edge, or improve customer service. Have coachees work in areas that are challenging and a stretch, but also let them achieve some small victories to boost morale and improve confidence in the process.

Throughout the coaching engagement, know that clear, consistent, meaningful, and frequent feedback is indispensable. (Please refer to Chapter Two for do's and don'ts of giving feedback.)

3. Follow-up.

Once the coaching engagement has ended, meet with the coachee informally every two to three months to review set goals as well as the coachee's progress and status in improving himself or herself.

The Value of Coaching

According to a report by Fortune magazine ("Executive Coaching—With Returns a CFO Could Love" by Anne Fisher, February 19, 2001), executives from large companies who had been coached by external coaches estimated the monetary payoff at about six times what the coaching had cost their companies. The executives also reported a boost in quantifiable job performance and better relationships with direct reports, bosses, peers, and clients. Finally, they cited increased job satisfaction and organizational commitment. Internal coaching by company executives may produce similar returns on investment.

Knowledgeable leaders bring tremendous value to an organization by turning their experience and expertise into guidance for those who

Sample Core Competencies for Emerging Leaders

The following list of competencies may be among the most vital for your organization's emerging talent. The first three are listed in order of importance — the ones that rise to the top of virtually every 360 Degree Feedback database nationwide — and the remaining fifteen are simply listed alphabetically:

Interpersonal skills (#1)
Relationship building
Communicating and informing
Effective conflict management
Coaching and mentoring (#2)
Influencing and motivating people (#3)
Adaptability
Building and managing a diverse workforce
Business acumen, finance
Change management
Cross-functional business knowledge
Creativity and innovation
Customer focus (internal and external)
Integrity and ethics
Project management
Organizational skills
Time management
Focus and follow-through
Strategic planning
Strategic thinking
Technology management

continued

Core Competenceies *continued from page 33*

Other fairly common core competencies your emerging leaders may be lacking include:

Thought leadership
    Demonstrates sound judgment
    Able to shape strategy
    Displays vision
    Drives global integration

People leadership
    Energizes the organization
    Develops organizational talent
    Ensures collaboration

Results leadership
    Strives towards organizational alignment
    Optimizes execution
    Drives organizational success
    Leads boldly and courageously

Personal leadership
    Earns and maintains trust of others
    Demonstrates agility and flexibility
    Has high integrity

seek to follow in their footsteps. At the same time, leaders themselves benefit from the process. In developing coaching skills, they learn to bond with their people while being given the chance to reflect on their own strengths and development areas, which in turn, leads to both personal and professional growth. In fact, the dual benefit of coaching makes it possible to distinguish an effective coaching model from an ineffective one—if the leader himself or herself is learning and changing along the way, the model is working.

Additional Resources

What Makes a Leader, by Daniel Goleman, Harvard Business Review, Product #3790, 1998.

Leadership That Gets Results, by Daniel Goleman, Harvard Business Review, Product #4487, 2000.

Why Should Anyone Be Led by You? by Daniel Goleman, Harvard Business Review, Product #5890, 2001.

Worksheet 1: Gaining Agreement on GAPS

Goals:	Abilities:
What does the coachee want to do (from his/her perspective)?	What can he or she do well (from his/her perspective)?
Perceptions:	**Standards:**
How do others see the coachee? How does the coach perceive his/her own performance?	What do you expect him or her to do? What does the organization need?

Worksheet 2:

Coach:	Purpose of partnership:
Coachee:	**Process:**
Date, time and place of initial meeting:	**Benefits:**
Coaching opportunity: • Assist in new job, role or prospect • Move from fully performing to exceeding expectations • Address a performance problem from lack of skill • Motivate this highly competent yet bored employee • Raise confidence to achieve tasks • Retain this high potential employee • Build new skills because of a corporate change • Establish coaching as mutual responsibility for growth *(Add others as necessary)*	**Roles/Responsibilities:**
Specific areas of focus: • Supporting/reinforcing a skill • Setting vision • Setting stretch goals • Training a new skill • Developing potential *(Add others as needed)*	**Next Steps:**

Worksheet 3: Action Plan

Behavior #1: I want to change or leverage more effectively:

Related Action Item #1:
Related Action Item #2:
Related Action Item #3:
Coachee's Comments:

How the coach will support the coachee in these endeavors:

Coach's Comments:

Behavior #2: I want to change or leverage more effectively:

Related Action Item #1:
Related Action Item #2:
Related Action Item #3:
Coachee's Comments:

How the coach will support the coachee in these endeavors:

Coach's Comments:

Behavior #3: I want to change or leverage more effectively:

Related Action Item #1:
Related Action Item #2:
Related Action Item #3:
Coachee's Comments:

How the coach will support the coachee in these endeavors:

Coach's Comments:

CHAPTER TWO
FEEDBACK—
The Breakfast of Champions

We must always change, renew, rejuvenate ourselves; otherwise we harden.
— Goethe

An estimated 50 percent of all performance problems occur because of lack of feedback. Management often complains that direct reports don't perform up to expectations, don't deliver quality results or don't have a clear idea of how to prioritize their long- and short-term tasks. At the same time, employees bemoan the fact that they are not given clear direction about expectations, time lines, priorities, and performance parameters. Complaints like these echo through the halls of corporations, large and small.

Yet, the solution to this dilemma is simple: clear, consistent, meaningful, and frequent feedback. Why then doesn't it happen? The reality is, on the receiving end, feedback is avoided because it's associated with feelings of embarrassment or even shame at being less than perfect. On the delivery end, bosses don't like to give feedback because they typically don't want to embarrass their direct reports. Further, many bosses are simply uncomfortable with giving feedback as it tends to make interactions a little too personal for their own comfort level. In turn, direct reports tend not to ask for feedback because they are afraid they might hear something unpleasant or that they may open the proverbial can of worms.

Actually, feedback is a healthy and necessary communication between leaders and their people. It reinforces competence and aligns expectations with the results needed to achieve business goals. Whatever reason may be preventing this open flow of much-needed guidance and direction on either side of the equation, all concerned have to move past it and see feedback for what it's designed and intended to be: a developmental opportunity.

In this chapter, readers will learn how to use a simple three-step process for delivering clear, consistent and frequent feedback, and why giving feedback is both a central component to any sound coaching engagement and a critical element to successful leadership and leadership development. Remember, it's not the job of HR to deliver feedback to employees; it's always the responsibility of the individual employee's manager. When feedback is delivered with sensitivity and clear purpose, it:

➤ Increases motivation and success

➤ Supports effective and efficient behavior

➤ Guides and puts individuals back on track

➤ Acts as a barometer to show where you stand

➤ Fills in knowledge gaps

➤ Aligns expectations and priorities

➤ Alleviates fear of the unknown

➤ Reinforces effective behavior

➤ Recognizes progress

➤ Offers encouragement

➤ Gives credit for achievement

The Basics of Feedback

1. What is feedback?
Feedback is a tool to deliver information regarding performance in a way that is non-judgmental and non-defensive. It's simply the sharing of information that moves people to action with the goal to improve.

2. What is the purpose of feedback?

➤ To improve someone's performance or take good performance to the next level

➢ To offer corrective guidance when people are making mistakes

➢ To let individuals know the consequences of their actions

➢ To discuss performance issues

3. When is it appropriate and ideal to give feedback?

➢ On a regular basis as part of a coaching engagement or simply throughout one's normal, day-to-day work

➢ Immediately after an interaction, task, project, or meeting

➢ When performance patterns appear (positive or negative)

➢ After a major initiative is complete

➢ Systematically throughout the year

➢ As part of the annual performance review process

4. Do's and Don'ts

➢ Do give feedback in a timely fashion—soon after you observe the behavior or action—good or bad.

➢ Do give feedback only in a one-on-one environment.

➢ Do give positive and negative information in every feedback situation. For every piece of "negative" feedback, give at least four pieces of "positive" feedback. Conventional wisdom commonly states a ratio of seven-to-one positive to negative as "the norm" (I think that ratio is a bit absurd). You're not a cheerleader or Mister Rogers Neighborhood, you are an executive charged with overseeing projects and the people who run them. A more realistic ratio, I believe, is three or four to one. Be encouraging but not patronizing. This keeps people motivated because they feel they are doing a good job. It keeps morale high because people won't feel like they are "always being criticized."

> ➤ Do not use feedback as an opportunity to blow off steam. It's meant to be constructive.
> ➤ Do not overwhelm the coachee by giving too much information; take up one or two issues at a time at most.

Give Constructive Feedback: A Three-Step Process

Step 1: Planning for Feedback

Be well prepared. Deliver feedback in a manner that ensures clarity and consistency. Follow a rational approach. Whether or not the feedback is part of a coaching engagement, prepare notes in advance of a feedback-giving meeting. Include specific examples of the behavior to be discussed—good or bad. Ask yourself the following questions:

> ➤ What is my reason for giving feedback?
> ➤ What is the business goal of giving this feedback?
> ➤ What specific action or behavior do I want to correct or reinforce?
> ➤ What are the consequences of this action or behavior?
> ➤ What is my reaction to the behavior or action? How am I impacted as a leader? How do I feel about it? How do others around the coachee feel about it?
> ➤ What behaviors or actions might be most motivating or important to change?
> ➤ What specific suggestions can I make that would help the coachee improve?
> ➤ What support can I offer going forward?

Step 2: Meeting to Deliver Feedback

Make sure feedback is delivered in private—initially, at least, until your team is strong with high trust—and, preferably, on your turf. Then, follow this seven-point feedback model:

1. Once the coachee is sitting with you, clearly state the purpose of your feedback: "Sue, I wanted to share a few thoughts with you about your performance on the Z Project that I know would be helpful to you..."

2. Describe specifically what action or behavior you observed: "Feedback, and my own observations, indicate that although you are moving things along ahead of schedule, team members feel as though you are doing so in a bit of a vacuum—not including them early on when decisions need to be made to move the project forward... I'm glad that you are so decisive; however, more inclusion will make things flow even smoother and make others feel even more a part of the entire process..."

3. Describe your reaction to what you observed (i.e., how you felt or how you were impacted by the coachee's actions or behaviors): "My concern is that when you leave others out, even me at times, it can look like 'The Susan Show' and we all know you better than that. Be sensitive to this feedback. Others, including me, feel left out..."

4. Give the coachee an opportunity to respond. Listen! Here is where you can also assess the coachee's readiness. How they respond to feedback says as much, if not more, than the feedback itself. I see this reaction to feedback as occurring on one of three levels, listed here in "descending order," worst-to-best:

   a. **Denial**—they can't accept the feedback so they simply deny that it's true.

   b. **Justification**—they "acknowledge" it but seem to have an excuse as to why it occurred. This is still denial, just a slightly refined version of it.

   c. **Acceptance**—here the receiver readily acknowledges the feedback as true and seeks to better understand where he or she went off the rails and wants your guidance to get back on track.

5. Develop an action plan or at least offer specific suggestions for improvement.

6. Summarize the conversation, touching on the key points— highs and lows—and offer your support and assistance.

7. Plan for a follow-up meeting to revisit the issue in 14–30 days or longer if warranted.

Feedback is different from other forms of dialogue between two people because it's an interchange of 70/30 or 80/20 rather than 50/50. In other words, your delivery of information to the coachee amounts from 70 to 80 percent of the communication; the coachee's response only accounts for 20 to 30 percent of the interchange.

If you have negative feedback to share, remember to begin with four positives. Make sure all feedback is based on accurate, unbiased information, but give the coachee the opportunity to respond in case he or she has more up-to-date or better information. If you have coachees who tend to defend or justify their behavior or performance, you may need to educate them on the constructive purpose of feedback or coach them on communication and listening skills (see Chapter Three). Don't argue. Don't be patronizing. Clarify your points. Be specific. Be direct.

Step 3: Follow-Up

Consistency is extremely important in the delivery of feedback. If the feedback is part of a continuing coaching engagement, proceed according to your established coaching plan. Support the coachee in his or her efforts to improve with reinforcement, encouragement, and coaching. If the feedback is not part of a coaching engagement, make sure you keep the follow-up meeting with the individual to revisit the issue; if necessary, schedule additional follow-ups.

Inspire Star Performers

The highest performers in an organization tend to be the most ignored group. They are the people who usually come in early, leave late, self-manage very effectively, and get the job done without constant prodding. Although praise may be offered on occasion, these high performers are seldom asked whether their work is challenging enough to keep their interest or is aligned with their career goals. They become "feedback-exempt" and, in time, this hurts them and the organization. In particular, when they no longer find their work challenging, they tend to leave for greener pastures—other business units (or other companies!) that have learned to leverage and further develop star performers.

Leaders who don't want to lose their best people need to know how to keep high performers motivated and inspired. In part, the solution is to offer consistent, constructive feedback regarding their performance, coupled with an inquiry as to how you can challenge and inspire them. Providing feedback and coaching such star performers is not only painless (since you are giving mostly positive feedback) but also essential. It's one of the many ways to groom emerging leaders and make your own job easier. When these high-performers stay rather than jump ship for new opportunities, the company preserves its knowledge base, skill, and expertise and enables you to plan for succession. Everyone wins!

Motivate Average Performers

In providing feedback to employees who perform from the low end of good to the high end of marginal, it's important to clearly and objectively outline corrective action. Some of the most common issues facing this group relate to attendance and quality of work output. The following scenario is an example of the application of feedback to such an issue.

"Karen" has been a manager in the apparel industry for about three years. She manages a key production area and, for the most part, her management skills are quite impressive; i.e., she gets accomplished what is expected of her. A review of her file shows that she has the promise of moving up, but her general tendency is to give just enough to get by. Over the past several months, she has continued to arrive at work later and later, ranging from ten to as many as thirty minutes, which has led to a decline in her team's motivation. Some of her workers are beginning to follow her example, as are some of her peers. If you are the executive to whom Karen reports, how would you deliver the necessary feedback?

Schedule a meeting with Karen, and once she is sitting with you, begin by stating the purpose of the meeting: "Karen, I want to address an issue of performance with you today. Let me share a few thoughts with you." Next, mention three to four positives. For example, "...over the past two years your management skills have grown and you have the promise of moving up. You have demonstrated an ability to move work through your area consistently on time, and the quality of output is high with little if any work coming back for rework." Next, specifically describe what you observed: "Yesterday, I saw you come in thirty minutes late for the third time this week." Next, describe your reaction: "I was surprised since you are usually fairly punctual." Give her an opportunity to respond: "Would you like to say anything about this?"

When giving feedback in such a situation, the employee may respond with one of three possible reactions as noted above: denial, justification, or accountability. If the employee denies the behavior in question or tries to justify it, it's important to listen rather than rebut or defend your position. Although admitting accountability is the preferred response, it often takes employees time to become confident that their jobs are not in jeopardy and that telling the truth is the expected norm. Giving feedback—both positive and negative—on a regular basis builds employees' trust in you and will help them be more accountable in the future.

After the employee has finished his or her response, proceed to the next step of offering specific suggestions for improvement: "If you are having car problems, perhaps you can join the company carpool or rideshare with a colleague." Be clear and direct with your suggestions. Be creative, too. Perhaps you can engage the employee in solving the problem with you. Be empathetic. The solution may require some flexibility on your part (changing schedules to accommodate a sick child, elder care, or other personal situations). Then, summarize the conversation, restating the issue and possible solutions discussed, and most important, offer your assistance, where possible, to get the problem solved. Remember, the goal is to solve the problem, improve performance, and move on. Finally, to close the meeting, schedule a follow-up session for a few weeks later, allowing enough time to observe the employee and review performance. The follow-up session should be structured similar to your first meeting. Start by reviewing the previous feedback and noting any observable changes; praise the employee for a job well done or offer additional feedback and corrective actions. Because Karen, the employee described in this example, is generally a very good manager, getting a handle on a visible issue such as punctuality can offer leverage in working toward "softer" issues that may be more difficult to measure, but more critical to moving up in the leadership ranks (e.g., communication skills, team-building, adaptability, creativity, etc.). The anticipated result is that she will increase her motivation and productivity in ways that matter both to her and to the organization as a whole. Further, not only are you offering her important feedback as well as corrective and constructive direction, you are also "modeling" for her how she, too, can better manage her own people should she encounter situations similar to her own.

Case Studies

Here are some examples of managers in need of feedback.

1. "Jacob" is a director known to everyone as a "hothead." He constantly blows off steam and tends to speak to people in a very condescending tone. At times, he belittles people in public regarding their performance or other issues. "Oh, that's just Jacob," is how some employees respond to his tirades. There is evidence, however, that morale is being affected. Draft your thoughts, reactions, and strategy for handling feedback with Jacob.

2. "Maria" is a fairly new manager, a little less than one year on the job. Although her skills are not superior, she always has a posi-

tive attitude and is tremendously motivated. She seems to consistently make every effort to "go the extra mile" as a way to improve her performance. However, she is short on some skills and makes mistakes. Draft your thoughts, reactions, and strategy as to how you would handle feedback with Maria.

3. "Sam" is an "old-timer" at the company with more than twenty years on the job. He is a very unassuming person, and a reliable, loyal hard worker who can always be counted on. Lately, however, his performance is slipping a bit and for no apparent reason. Although the reasons for his recent slippage are not obvious, draft your thoughts, reactions, and strategy as to how you would handle feedback with Sam. Is straight feedback called for here or rather inquiry?

Feedback and Rewards

Never offer empty promises related to a job well done. If employees perform to your expectations, they will expect rewards and you'll be expected to deliver. Keep promises realistic, and manage employees' expectations. Doing so builds further trust in you as a leader, generates loyalty to the organization, and increases motivation and performance. Offer consistent feedback to all employees. If corrective action is necessary, encourage employees to take such action as a way to assist them in their goals to move up in the company.

In addition, be open to asking for and receiving feedback from those to whom you report. You may be surprised at the response. Let's face it, as I stated in the first chapter of the book, in this process no one is exempt from learning, not even you as the executive or executive-as-coach. Being proactive in seeking out feedback is critical to your own success even if you may be in the "sunset" of your career. If you are serious about stretching yourself further, introduce "open feedback" to your team and be open to receiving their feedback as well. Don't tolerate "suck-ups" and also do not encourage "bashing"—you set the tone for such openness and honesty. Blaze this trail with confidence and clarity, and the results will benefit everyone.

One of the roles of leaders is to let people know how they are doing—good or bad. If you don't tell people how they are doing, they will assume that they are doing a good job. The ultimate goal of feedback is to help people understand themselves better so they can improve and grow. Particularly with coachees who have leadership potential, it's important to serve as a role model in showing how good feedback is delivered. In turn, they can use it with their teams and as the leaders of the future. When delivered effectively, feedback is a strategic tool to increase the overall effectiveness of individuals, teams, business units, and companies as a whole.

Case Study:
It's Not About Right or Wrong; It's About Perception

A favorite senior executive client of mine entered the management ranks of a large western power utility company as a nuclear scientist at one of its nuclear power plants. After ten years, he left the power plant to take a more senior position at the parent company. In 2005, he was further promoted to senior vice president of Generation Operations to lead the entire business unit. The unit covered not just the nuclear power plant, but all areas used in the production of electricity for one of the nation's largest power utilities covering an area of 45,000 square miles.

Styles clash. When he was subsequently returned to the power plant and other related responsibilities, he realized his leadership style was completely different from that of the retiring senior officer he was replacing. Four vice presidents who ran the plant and now reported directly to him also observed the significant difference in style. In fact, his style was so different from his predecessor's that he saw a significant challenge ahead in leading these four VPs as well as the entire business unit.

"I realized there was a need for significant operational, organizational, and cultural change to bring the organization and its leaders up to a level they had once achieved earlier in their history—operating what was once the top-rated nuclear power plant in America," he observed. "The four vice presidents had extremely different personalities and working styles. They did not work together well, nor did they have a very high level of trust with each other."

His own leadership style was, for the most part, a collaborative one. He pushed responsibility onto those who worked for him, expecting high performance at all times. He also required subordinates to stretch beyond the nominal role they were typically accustomed to playing—quite the opposite tack that his predecessor took. His goal was to develop a team that could work together effectively and provide unified leadership, managing strategy, planning, and execution of the company's goals. Period.

He brought my team and I in to coach the vice presidents—and the senior executive himself—to get them all to work with each other more effectively. Using 360 Degree Feedback instruments, coupled with interviews and extensive observations of the leadership team, we tailored an executive coaching program to each vice president's strengths and opportunities for growth.

The feedback session. First, the coach gave coachees a detailed summary of their 360 assessment in a two-hour session that also included our assessment specialist. The coach covered all strengths and developmental opportunities identified by the assessment. But most importantly, each feedback session was not just a "data dump" based on scores alone. Rather, it was a very dynamic meeting and left ample room for the delivery of news, good and bad, as well as responses by the coachee. The coach guided the coachee in understanding the scores and any behavioral patterns emerging from the third-party feedback. However, rather than allowing the coachee to justify or defend behaviors, the coach encouraged the coachee to see any negative comments through the eyes of the 360 survey respondent. If the coachee became defensive, the coach would say: "True or not, just try to understand why someone might see you that way." Coachees need to learn to appreciate the perceptions of others whether they agree with them or not, because that perception is hurting them. It's not about right or wrong; it's about perception. The feedback round concluded with the coach and coachee meeting with the boss to also highlight areas of strengths and developmental opportunity. This fostered a high degree of transparency in the process and sent a message to everyone involved that they were in this for development with no exceptions.

Industrial marriage counseling. Coaching assignments involved one-on-one sessions in different settings and situations. The coach also took the vice presidents on several off-site, half-day executive development forums to discuss and resolve interpersonal issues that had been barriers to effective collaboration. My client referred to these off-site executive development forums as "industrial marriage counseling." The lesson here is that the work done was just as beneficial to the executive in charge as it was to those being coached at the levels below him. It helped all become better managers, leaders, and coaches themselves as they progressed through the process. All concerned had a great need to not only change, but to learn how to change and how to develop an environment of high trust among themselves and in their respective areas of responsibility, in order to be more effective.

"Through the assessment process and initial coaching work with the vice presidents, it became apparent that the leadership issues ran deeper within the organization," the executive was heard saying. "We decided to take the initiative one level deeper in the organization to fourteen managers. These managers run the day-to-day operations of the plant and report to the vice presidents. Now, with the entire leadership and management team being coached concurrently, it gave us a considerable edge in transforming a number of old bad habits, allowing our team to strive toward higher performance and productivity."

True change. However, the goal was never to create identical leaders. Rather, it was to assist several distinctly different individuals to work together utilizing their differences, enabling them to make better decisions than any of them could make individually. Similarly, the goal was not to "clone" the next level of managers to be like their bosses, but rather help them individually to find their place of strength and effectiveness to support the vice presidents. "It's remarkable to see people who have worked together for twenty years starting to deal with each other in a demonstrably different way and visibly appreciate the differences among themselves," he said. "Others who have known them see them getting along and making an effort, and it's a very powerful exercise for others to see. When leaders role-model the culture and values they want the organization to have, reflecting what they have learned and believe in, it presents a powerful message to the entire organization."

The legacy. In 2008, when the senior executive retired, to his credit, he had identified a successor and worked vigorously to promote that person. He now had a legacy of success and succession to leave behind. The new leader glided into the senior role with a team that may have needed some further development, but had already made significant leaps forward. The road to the next generation of leaders had become clearer and easier to see.

Additional Resources

"Fear of Feedback" by Jay M. Jackman and Myra H. Strober, *Harvard Business Review*, www.harvardbusiness.org, Product No. R0304H, 2003.

"Feedback That Works" by Cynthia Morrison Phoel, Harvard Business Review, www.harvardbusiness.org, Product No. U0902A, 2009.

"CEO's Six Steps to Effective Feedback" by Christina Bielaszka-Du-Vernay, *Harvard Business Review*, www.harvardbusiness.org, Product No. U0708A, 2007.

The One Minute Manager by Kenneth H. Blanchard, Ph.D. and Spencer Johnson, M.D., William Morrow, September 1982.

CHAPTER THREE
MAKING COMMUNICATION WORK

Communication is everyone's panacea for everything.

— Tom Peters

When coaching or mentoring emerging leaders, excellent communication skills are essential, including active listening and delivering effective feedback. Communication skills are also the foundation for other skills discussed later in this book. To motivate and influence people, *leaders must communicate a vision, mission, or goal with clarity and passion.* That's how one effectively mentors followers. Effective communication is also crucial in developing and nurturing relationships across all levels of an organization, and here, the amount and style of communication needs to be appropriate to the people being addressed, whether superiors, peers, subordinates, or other stakeholders. The most common complaints made by both leaders and their subordinates revolve around the failure of individuals in their organization to communicate meaningful information in a lucid manner. And, as may be no surprise to you, 80-plus percent of the work that competent coaches and consultants do in large organizations revolves not around systems or other "fixes," but rather around the need to dramatically improve overall communication.

While poor communication is a problem at all levels of an organization, change needs to be initiated from the top. After all, since a leader's job is to shape a vision for the enterprise, develop a strategy from it, and motivate others to execute it, a leader needs to articulate the vision and strategy clearly. Without clarity, people cannot be expected to take responsibility or be held wholly accountable for the actions required to move that strategy from abstraction into reality.

Leaders who can't articulate their ideas will always have problems with execution. If the direction is not crystal clear, people don't know where to go. Important issues and items tend to fall through the cracks when people don't understand what is expected of them. Clearly, leaders must be excellent communicators, but in many cases, that skill alone will not push the organization forward if deeper problems exist. Poor communication is often a symptom of a dysfunctional corporate culture, and unless those underlying issues are addressed, changes in communication styles will amount to little more than window dressing.

Is It a Question of Trust?

In the vast majority of corporate environments where "poor communication" is a common complaint, the problem stems from one of two sources:

1. A lack of basic communication skills—both speaking and listening—among people in the organization.

2. A climate of fear in which people are simply afraid to speak their minds or to give feedback to those who are poor communicators.

Of these, the latter (#2) is a much more serious problem. Even people with a relatively low level of communication skills can manage effectively enough as long as trust is high. The culture of such organizations encourages people to feel comfortable making mistakes; the underlying assumption of such an environment expresses confidence in each individual's ability, in the end, to arrive at an effective solution or result. However, where trust is lacking, even the most highly skilled communicators fall silent. Creating an atmosphere that creates trust is the primary and paramount task in improving communication. Here's what such an environment looks like:

➤ People are encouraged to be candid and honest, to be themselves, and to state what is true for them from their point of view. There is a prevailing lack of pretense in the organization. Individuals are comfortable being "vulnerable" or open.

➤ People communicate openly, honestly, and with integrity. Agendas (hidden or otherwise), posturing, putting on airs, or grabbing the limelight are noticeably absent. People state the facts (as they see them) without fear of retribution and freely challenge one another in a positive manner that benefits everyone.

➤ Communication is concise, specific, and unambiguous. Mistrust is bred in companies where everyone speaks in broad, vague generalities (it's amazing that anything is accomplished in such organizations!). Cutting through ambiguity can be as simple as asking direct questions, such as: "What does that mean?", "Where did those numbers come from?", or "What's behind those statistics?" Assertive, persistent, cut-to-the chase questions are a powerful antidote to hedging, soft-pedaling, and gobbledygook.

➤ People invite feedback and are willing to accept it openly without defensiveness, excuses, denial, or justifications.

➤ Feedback is offered openly, honestly, and without agenda. Effective feedback is always constructive, respectful, compassionate, and never personal.

➤ Individuals feel safe enough to tell the truth. Think for a moment about how profound a statement that is. In such organizations, there is no need to explain away mistakes or make excuses. An environment of trust has no room for the "blame game."

➤ Accountability is a badge of honor throughout the organization. Emerging leaders are not afraid to tell the truth, even if it's bad news. After all, if the bad news is hidden from the boss, the problem cannot be corrected and everyone looks bad. Openly sharing bad news gives everyone an opportunity to improve operations. Good communication promotes trust, which in turn, fosters loyalty. On the other hand, when mistrust is rampant, communication will remain poor or non-existent. In such an environment, addressing the communication skills of individuals will be a losing battle for even the best coach.

What's Your Communication Style?

Some companies, on the other hand, have cultures in which trust and open, honest communication abound but nonetheless struggle with other organizational problems. In those situations, deficient individual communication skills may be at the root of their organizational problems. Some indicators to watch for include:

> ➢ The same problems continue to arise, even after potential solutions are found

> ➢ A noticeable lack of rapport between members of a team

> ➢ Communication breakdowns occur frequently

> ➢ Decreasing sales because people miss key customer issues

> ➢ Failures in production due to miscommunication

> ➢ Employees expect their leaders to solve all the organization's problems

To remedy such situations, leaders need to be open and willing to improve their own communication skills. Only by understanding and appreciating the individual differences in communication styles—including their own—will they be able to effectively coach their subordinates in a way that exhibits flexibility.

Substandard or poor communicators usually fall into one of four categories:

1. **Egotistic.** People with abnormally large egos tend to talk too much and rarely listen. I refer to them as "raging extroverts." Secure in the (mistaken) belief that they know it all, there is no room for input or improvement. By contrast, sometimes an inflated ego is also accompanied by an inner sense of insecurity. In these cases, the problem is they don't talk enough for the simple reason that they don't want to

share their precious information. This type I would refer to as "raging introverts."

2. **Unfocused.** Some executives have short attention spans, are distracted, or just unfocused. They jump from topic to topic, ramble too much, or lack the clarity of expression required to lead, inspire, influence, and motivate.

3. **Extroverted.** Enthusiasm is a wonderful thing, but these overly outgoing executives really overdo it, often short-circuiting others with too much information. They leave the listener feeling simply overwhelmed

4. **Wallflowers.** These shy, introverted people prefer not to talk or they take a "minimalist" approach. This trait is particularly common among executives who were promoted on the basis of scientific or technical expertise and are simply uncomfortable—sometimes excruciatingly so—in social settings and general interactions with others.

Although correlations between communication style and personality are obvious, particularly in terms of the Myers-Briggs dichotomy of introverts versus extroverts, innate personality is neither a prerequisite for being a leader nor an excuse for being a poor communicator in a leadership position. Case in point, a USA Today article titled "Not all successful CEOs are extroverts" by Del Jones (June 7, 2006) observed that Bill Gates, Warren Buffett, Charles Schwab, Steven Spielberg, and Sara Lee CEO Brenda Barnes are a few of the many examples of leaders who are uncomfortable in social settings, yet manage to control and even harness their introverted nature on the job. "Introverts," according to SkyeTec CEO Chris Uhland, "say they succeed because they have inner strength and think before they act. When faced with difficult decisions, introverts worry little about what other people will think of them." They will rely more on their inner dialogue (data) than the external dialogue as extroverts often do. Again, neither style nor preference is right; they are simply different. When used effectively, preference does not matter so long as the communications are clear and understood by the listener.

In his 2001 bestseller, *Good to Great: Why Some Companies Make the Leap... and Other's Don't* (HarperBusiness), Jim Collins, similarly dispelled the accepted wisdom that successful leaders are all naturally outgoing or charismatic. In fact, he observed that the most successful companies had self-effacing and humble CEOs. Of course, don't take this as a blanket endorsement of introverts as leaders; they have their problems, too! An introverted nature, in fact, may well have contributed to leadership errors on the part of former Enron CEO Jeffrey Skilling, a shy, inhibited loner who was referred to as antisocial by those close to him. The simple truth is that leaders are paid to lead. Since it's impossible to motivate and inspire people without communicating with them, leaders should make the acquisition of excellent communication skills a top priority. It's an investment that pays many benefits because those skills also support other leadership competencies addressed in this book. When is the best time to acquire these skills? As soon as possible, under the guidance of an experienced, competent leader, or coach—even including self as coach, if the commitment to grow exists within you.

To assess an emerging leader's communication skills in preparation for coaching, a 360 Degree Feedback instrument (preferably administered in cooperation with one's HR department) is an essential tool. Based on input from people surrounding the emerging leader, this evaluation method reveals strengths and deficiencies in the area of communication effectiveness, specifically:

1. How much the individual communicates (quantity—too much or not enough)
2. What is communicated (content)
3. How it's communicated (style or quality)

Although leaders cannot be expected to be expert in the nuances of each personality type and their associated communication styles, at a minimum, they should understand their own style and communication challenges. From that self-knowledge will come a gradual awareness

Moving a Coachee from "Incompetence" or Mere "Competence" to Mastery

With each skill that one coaches, four levels of learning can be observed. In order to acquire mastery of a subject, a coachee moves up through the following levels one by one:

1. Unconscious incompetence
2. Conscious incompetence
3. Conscious competence
4. Unconscious competence

The first level is unconscious incompetence. At this level, a coachee lacks a skill or critical knowledge, but is not aware of that fact. As coachees begin to receive instruction, they move to the second level, conscious incompetence. They are now aware that they lack the skill and need to improve. This is the most challenging and time-consuming coaching stage. It requires a great deal of instruction, practice, feedback, and support from the mentor. Success in that stage leads to the next level, conscious competence. Here, the coachee applies the skill, but it does not come naturally—they must think about it while actually performing it. With continued practice, the level of unconscious competence is reached. In this culminating level of achievement, the coachee has mastered the skill and practices it naturally without thinking about it.

(The earliest origin of this theory of four levels of competence is not known although course developers at Gordon Training International have played a role in defining it and promoting its use.)

of and sensitivity to the varied personality types and communication styles of their peers and subordinates. And with those vital pieces in place, they can then better target their communications to lead, inspire, motivate, and influence.

Please note that the 360 feedback measures far more than just communication style. But for the sake of this particular topic, strong emphasis is added here about communication. (Refer to the Appendix for details on this assessment tool and process.)

Quick Tips for Improving Communication Skills

Here are a few quick tips for immediate application to the workplace, based on the most common communication shortcomings observed in leaders.

Problem: An emerging leader overwhelms direct reports and others with too much information.

Coach the individual to:

➤ Prioritize and group thoughts in advance. Suggest a "headline communication" approach in which the main idea (the headline) is presented first, followed by no more than two to three pieces of supporting information.

➤ Stop talking! Allow time for those critically important "headlines" to sink in, even if there are other details one would like to share.

➤ Create a time and safe space for reflection and dialogue. Encourage listeners to digest the information and ask questions to get a better sense of the listeners' level of comprehension (and agreement or disagreement). The answers to these questions will most likely cover any additional information one wants to communicate. If not, those points can be covered later, but only on an as-needed basis.

➤ Check in with one's listeners frequently. Are they tracking or not? Rather than asking, "Is this clear?" (which invites a yes/no answer and can be demeaning), practice asking open-ended questions, such as "How can I clarify this further?" or "What needs more explanation?"

➢ Avoid emotionally charged appeals. Stay focused on making a point from a well-reasoned and thoughtful perspective. Don't come at the communication as if it were a sales pitch to "close the deal" or win someone over.

➢ Handle interruptions gracefully. When one's presentation is interrupted, don't take it personally. Avoid the temptation to dismiss such interruptions with a terse "Excuse me, I haven't finished yet." Interruption can be used to improve communication and converted into valuable learning experiences. For example, an interruption could be a hint from listeners that one is rambling, has gone on too long, or that another person has something important to add. In either case, steamrolling over an interruption is rarely, if ever, productive. Instead, use the interruption to engage and lead a conversation; one can always take the floor again at a later time.

➢ Respond, don't react. When one's presentation is interrupted—perhaps by questions—or otherwise knocked off track, take a deep breath, relax, and stay calm. Rather than rushing into a habit-based, emotional reaction that might be hurtful or counterproductive, use that interval to compose an emotionally balanced and thoughtful response. Practice buying time with lead-ins like, "Let me reflect on that for a moment" or "Allow me to think out loud here for a moment" or "Perhaps we can return to the previous topic or point if no one else needs to weigh in."

Problem: An emerging leader "intimidates" direct reports (this is a very subjective issue).

Coach the individual to:

➢ First, be open to the differing styles of direct reports and how they absorb and deliver information themselves. Those that are more "shy" will perceive anything "strong" as intimidation or feel overwhelmed. Stronger personality types will perceive "softer" communications as being too soft, vague, and downright ineffective. Balance and flexibility are keys to success here.

➤ Be humble or at least unassuming. An individual's communication skills should be viewed as a special gift for the greater good, never as a weapon or for one-upmanship.

➤ "Surrender" to co-communicators. It's impossible to communicate effectively while at the same time being "armed for battle." Leaders communicate best when they know, deep within themselves, they are in control of the process and that other people can cause no irreparable harm. Surrendering means being fully present in the moment and letting go of one's agenda (hidden or otherwise). Effective leaders are aware of and honor their own strong personal feelings and fears, but they aren't ruled by them. This kind of personal and managerial maturity takes a great deal of serious inner work. It's all about finding a place of grounding that enables one to fully hear the content and feelings behind another person's message and one's own.

➤ Utilize the technique of active listening. (See page ?) Coachees can practice this skill one-on-one with a coach or in groups.

➤ Don't be afraid to show one's "human" side. Many executives are naturally warm and charming, but hide that personality for fear that others might take advantage. It's part of the paradox of control: the more you have, the more you can give away.

➤ Phrase opinions judiciously and with sensitivity. Avoid being blunt or strident. Add equivocating words or pose questions when expressing strong opinions.

➤ Variety improves communication. Top baseball pitchers and jazz musicians know the value of "mixing things up." Follow their lead by varying one's rhetorical, persuasive, and influencing styles throughout a specific presentation or speech. Avoid being a "Johnny One-Note." It's not necessary to always be assertive; in fact, it can be very counterproductive.

➤ Loosen up! Have fun, or at least fake it until you make it! Listeners relax when they sense the speaker (or leader) is enjoying the ride, too. Study after study shows that when people are having a bit of fun in a presentation (maybe even laughing from time to time), they remember much more of the content. If one is by nature a bit nervous with public speaking, this will take some time. It's a journey and it helps to visualize the direction in which one wants to go. Start by imagining a relaxed, unpretentious setting where one is surrounded by friends who unconditionally accept each other exactly as they are. These guidelines are true for large-scale presentations as well as staff meetings.

➤ Get to know each other as people. Schedule informal get-togethers (e.g., "Breakfast with Jane") as a way of allowing people to become comfortable with each other. Help the coachee understand that attendance may be sparse in the beginning. It often takes some time for people to realize that it's "safe" to attend. A good way to break the ice is to encourage the coachee to begin the process by inviting smaller groups (five to seven people perhaps, or even less). This will immeasurably help lower the intimidation factor. Follow that with a series of "voluntary attendance" get-togethers and see who shows up. Another variation would be to start the process with specially created focus groups charged with discussing topics of concern to the business unit, set in an open environment for the purpose of brainstorming.

Problem: An emerging leader is too timid in his or her communication (this, too, is very subjective).

Again, flexibility on the part of the leader is key to success. **Coach the individual to utilize active listening skills to:**

➢ Say exactly what he or she means. Help coachees identify exactly what specific fears are blocking them in this regard. This will require intimate, trust-based mentorship of a very high order, indeed, and is worth every ounce of energy spent.

➢ Don't hedge. Speak succinctly, without the use of qualifiers and unnecessary words. Be specific and explain the reasons behind your words. For example, rather than saying, "I think we made the right decision," encourage one's coachee to say, "We made the right decision because this initiative is in line with our long-term expansion goals." Instead of this: "I like the way you handled that customer complaint," try this: "You not only handled the customer complaint, but got a referral to another prospect."

➢ Use concise communication to set clear boundaries and areas of responsibility. Timid and insecure coachees tend to take on other people's problems or substandard performance as their own—a tendency often perpetuated by deficient communication skills, i.e., an unwillingness or inability to express displeasure with another's performance. Here's a typical example: "I had to handle that problem with the customer myself because Jorge didn't know what to do." Suggestion: Encourage one's coachee to throw that baggage right back where it truly belongs (heads up, Jorge by saying something like this: "Jorge appears unable to handle customer complaints and requires additional training and feedback to that effect." People begin to set healthy boundaries (on the job and in their personal lives) when they are able to verbalize their wishes and expectations clearly.

Problem: An executive sounds unfocused or disorganized in meetings.

Coach the individual to:

➢ Prepare thoughts in advance of meetings. Write out notes in headline form that allow improvisation around one's essential points. It creates a more relaxed environment and helps the presenter exude greater confidence rather than taking a rigid or "scripted" approach.

➢ Find one's center (sense of confidence). Take a moment (and a few slow, deep breaths) to become centered before beginning to speak, always.

➢ Use a crisp, concise, and succinct communication style. Focus on clearly stating one's goals, objectives, progress, and concerns.

➢ Slow down when delivering. Speed and volume actually impede communication. Clarity of expression, a relaxed pace, and conciseness of thought increases people's understanding.

➢ Keep it simple. Convey at most, one or two ideas at a time.

➢ Stay focused but flexible. Focus is vital, of course, but needs to be balanced with attentiveness to cues from others, subtle or otherwise, signaling a need for greater flexibility. Be willing to modify the agenda, answer questions, address concerns, and enter into a positive give-and-take sharing of ideas "on the fly."

➢ Move from the general to the specific. Begin with a mile-high overview, particularly when reporting to senior management. After outlining the big picture, move to specifics. Editorialize by adding an opinion, using words such as "I think...", "We recommend...", "This is very good news...", or "This is a big concern."

➢ Curiosity is contagious and healthy; encourage it by using it. Ask questions to maximize the listeners' understanding. When the speaker expresses curiosity by actively engaging the audience with relevant questions, it encourages listeners to do the same and raises the overall "alertness" factor in the room. People retain more when they feel engaged in the process. Asking questions—either rhetorically or of specific individuals—also sends a positive message that the speaker doesn't have all the answers. This is a good thing. People who act like they know it all usually don't.

Active Listening

Communication is a two-way street—it involves speaking and listening. It's surprising how many otherwise intelligent executives just don't understand that. Many leaders who are skilled at expressing themselves clearly and articulately are often deficient when it comes to listening (although they'd be loathe to admit it). What they've actually become skilled at is appearing to listen to someone else, while their mind feverishly formulates and rehearses their own response. It's a very common human trait, especially in highly competitive organizations. People often feel that if they don't insert a response, they'll miss their chance to speak their mind and lose their moment in the sun.

Other people fall into a different trap when listening: their mind wanders. In today's world, where multitasking and short attention spans are seemingly the norm, it's shockingly easy to find oneself miles away, thinking of something other than what the speaker is presenting. (It happens to everybody from time to time). Worse yet are the folks who claim to be able to "listen" to a third person on the cell phone while also "listening" to someone sitting across from them. These poor listeners miss at least 80 percent of the message, as recent research indicates: their responses to the speaker are almost guaranteed to be out of sync (often comically so). In group workshop situations, multitasking participants often laugh at themselves when they become aware of how irrelevant their carefully rehearsed responses were to the actual message being delivered in real-time. Once they take the time to understand the point the speaker is making, their response becomes moot. Many conflicts and problems could be avoided or solved by more effective, active listening—being fully present, in the moment and fully engaged.

Listening is a way of deepening one's understanding of another person's thoughts. This is accomplished through active listening—not just hearing, but also intently concentrating on the person who is speaking and the message they're communicating. Active listening promotes learning and relevant responses; in fact, it's the only way to accomplish those vitally important goals. The four steps of active listening for your benefit and the benefit of the coachee are:

1. Open your mind and truly listen. It may take many hours of practice to stop rehearsing a response while listening, or to resist the temptation to let the mind wander.

2. Clarify understanding. Ask the speaker all the questions necessary to truly understand what is being said. Ask who, what, where, when, and how. Avoid, if possible, asking why. "Why" does not ask for specific details and may make the speaker defensive; it's often perceived as a challenge, not an inquiry.

3. Acknowledge. Communicate that the speaker is being heard, that their message is being fully understood, and that you, the listener, are fully engaged. One doesn't necessarily have to agree with the content of the speaker's message to accomplish this. Listening is an opening-up experience, not a debate. Use expressions such as: I understand. Please continue. Thank you for telling me. I've got that. I'm glad you told me. I appreciate your input. Incorporate affirming the "I'm listening" body language as well, such as nodding one's head.

4. Repeat back. Use a short paraphrase to summarize what the speaker said. It's an excellent way to demonstrate one's understanding of the message. Here again, agreement is not necessary on the part of the listener, just an understanding of the speaker's message. This also creates a valuable space in which the speaker can correct any misunderstandings.

Creating Rapport

Rapport, according to Jim Peal, Ph.D., President of the Leadership Development Group (Oakland, California, www.LeadershipDG.com), may be understood as a cycle with three components: Calibration, Pacing, and Leading. In any interaction, Peal says, one first needs to calibrate, which requires conscious attention to the communication methods the other person is using. This includes visual cues, such as facial expression, body posture, and gestures, along with auditory cues, including tone of voice, tempo, and key words and phrases. "Key words" are the verbal equivalent of underlined or italicized written text. They are often accompanied by a gesture, a dramatic pause, or are framed in such a way as to create an emotional charge around them.

Research in neurolinguistic programming, says Peal, demonstrates a stunning conclusion: only about 7 percent of the responses elicited by one's communication are caused by the content of one's message. Thirty-eight percent comes from how the words are spoken, along with other vocal information. Fifty-five percent comes from body language. That's why it's so critical to calibrate nonverbal cues.

After calibration, the second step in creating rapport is to pace the other individual. That means matching and mirroring one's communication behavior to the other person's tone of voice, body language, key words, and emotional intensity. It's critical to do so in a non-mimicking way, lest the speaker feel they're being ridiculed. Pacing, which matches the other person's visual and verbal cues, helps create a comfortable, warm, and human connection with the other individual. From that point, one is in a much better position to lead the communication to a desired outcome.

Peal suggests the following openers to create rapport:

"Help me understand..."

"I'm wondering about..."

"This may seem like an obvious question..."

"I'm curious about..."

For more detailed tips on active listening, refer to Chapter Five in the section titled: "Practice tips for a coachee who needs to develop better listening skills."

It All Comes Down to Communication

According to the Center for Creative Leadership, 82 percent of new leaders fail to build good relationships with peers and subordinates, and 58 percent experience confusion or uncertainty about what the boss expects. In most cases, these deficiencies result from poor communication. Sometimes the root cause is an organization that lacks an environment of trust and openness. In other situations, problems arise at the individual level, notably when emerging leaders are left to their own devices instead of being coached to become better communicators. Communication really could be a panacea for everything—as Tom Peters famously says—if it were only given a chance.

Additional Resources

Introduction to Type and Communication by Donna Dunning. CPP, Inc., www.cpp.com, Mountain View, CA 2003.

Unlimited Power: The New Science of Personal Achievement by Anthony Robbins, Free Press, 1997.

Daring to Have Real Conversations in Business by James (Jim) Peal, Ph.D., Leadership Development Group, 2009.

Fierce Conversations: Achieving Success at Work and in Life One Conversation at a Time by Susan Scott, Berkley Trade, Reprint Edition, 2004.

Crucial Conversations: Tools for Talking When Stakes Are High by Kerry Patterson et al., McGraw-Hill, 2002.

The Five Dysfunctions of a Team: A Leadership Fable by Patrick Lencioni, Jossey-Bass, 2002.

Leadership and Self Deception: Getting Out of the Box by Arbinger Institute, Berrett-Koehler Publishers, 2002.

CHAPTER FOUR
THE ART OF MANAGING CONFLICT

He who seeks vengeance must dig two graves: one for his enemy and one for himself.
— Chinese Proverb

One of the paradoxes of American life is that in our conflict-ridden society, so few people know how to effectively deal with it. Executives are no exception; far too many of them lack even the most basic conflict-resolution skills. Like most other people in the United States, they deal with disputes the old-fashioned way: by sheer avoidance or head-on. When conflict-related issues are not resolved, the remaining loose ends undermine relationships and damage group cohesiveness. Unmanaged, open-ended conflict often turns into gossip and toxic third-party chatter, which can keep the fire burning for weeks, months, and even longer. The results are low morale and ineffective people. In terms of an organization's productivity, unmanaged conflict is akin to running a race with shoelaces tied to one other. It lurks under the surface, hard to see but ever-present, limiting and eventually tripping up executives and others as they attempt to move the organization forward in the race for success.

This chapter defines the scope of the problem and offers practical tools to develop balanced conflict management skills. The goal is for dissention to be addressed in real time—before it escalates. Mentors and coachees will learn how to create clarity around diverging viewpoints and balance varied approaches to problem solving. Even more importantly—and surprisingly—it will be shown how disagreement among individuals can be used as a powerful tool to advance productivity.

Avoid or Attack?

Whether in business, civic, or personal life, conflict is ubiquitous. It's important to accept that, at this stage of societal and human development, conflict is a widespread phenomenon. That basic fact can't be changed. However, a leader's power and influence come into play regarding how an individual or organization deals with these inevitable disagreements among people. Strategies vary from avoidance to head-on collision and all the points in-between. Which of the following conflict-related "snapshots" apply to your organization and culture?

> ➤ When a tough problem arises, individuals and teams tend to avoid conflict.

> ➤ Some individuals seem to create conflict wherever they go.

> ➤ Certain people bulldoze over diverging opinions, while others tend to give in, even when they disagree.

> ➤ The typical team meeting is largely a matter of polite conversation over "tea and crumpets" that leaves the tough issues unresolved.

> ➤ Group discussions center around debating opinions, predictions, and subjective viewpoints with little or no actual operational or external data on the table.

> ➤ Teams debate the pros and cons of only two alternative courses of action rather than considering multiple possible scenarios.

> ➤ There are clear winners and losers following team meetings.

> ➤ The workplace is a tense environment with little humor or shared social activity.

> ➤ Decisions made at the top give little attention to diverging viewpoints.

> ➤ Junior executives have little authority to make decisions even within their own departments.

Even the best organizations have occasional problems like the ones listed above. However, when the list represents a systemic norm rather than an isolated exception, immediate steps are needed to improve conflict management skills.

One of the first steps is to actively promote the transfer of conflict management skills from the executive levels and downward. Executives often do a decent job of managing conflict among their direct reports, but the effort frequently stops there. While subordinates may acknowledge their leader's help in resolving issues at the top levels, they are probably complaining privately that the boss doesn't want to hear about their teams' problems. When leaders model effective and thoughtful conflict management skills, subordinates recognize the benefits of those approaches. With the right coaching, they, in turn, can begin to model those successful behaviors within their own group, team, or business unit. Balanced conflict management—coached by an organization's leaders—creates an environment of trust at all levels where people feel safe dealing with conflict.

What is a balanced approach to managing conflict? It's neither "marriage counseling" nor mortal combat. Rather, it's an impartial and equitable approach to addressing issues in real time—the ultimate aim of which is to achieve clarity and find common ground among diverging ideas and viewpoints. The goal is not to reach total agreement among all parties, but find an understanding on which to base further action. Clarity is always more important than resolution, because the collective stakeholders of an organization need to know exactly where they stand today before they can move forward. Agreement actually comes second to clarity as it should.

Prevention: the Best "Cure" for Unproductive Conflict

One of the most common sources of unproductive organizational conflict is competition among employees and junior executives for resources, the spotlight, advancement, or the boss's attention. And even though they probably won't admit it, most executives have the same desire to be seen and heard. In staff meetings around the country each day, untold numbers of people at all levels are focused on two objectives: impressing an influential superior and using a report or presentation to position themselves as the hero or heroine of the day. In the best case, such ego-driven behavior is just a waste of ingenuity. The worst-case scenario happens when someone in the group promotes an opposing point of view. Then, watch out for the fireworks! The meeting is very likely to deteriorate into snips, backhanded compliments, mild sarcasm, and even teasing. Unless a cool-headed executive quickly reins in such behavior, watch for it to escalate into caustic comments, strong language, verbal abuse, and shouting matches.

There are some proactive steps that leaders can take to stop unproductive conflicts from arising in the first place. Here are some very effective ones:

➢ Clearly articulate the roles, responsibilities, and expectations of all staff. Reinforce those messages regularly. Ambiguity creates a powerful breeding ground for conflict because people make assumptions that are either erroneous or in direct conflict with others.

➢ Balance team assignments based on "chemistry" and skill. Choosing the "best and brightest" may sound ideal for a high-powered problem-solving team, but it's usually not. If they happen to be the biggest egos, the fiercest warriors, or the most opinionated people in the company, their constant competition for airtime, recognition, and success may spell disaster. Instead, assemble teams with a balanced blend of personalities and skill sets. Reinforce the importance of collaboration and cooperation as a group value. Don't put together a team composed of a single personality type, be they "drivers," idea people, introverted number-crunchers, or go-getters. Make it your business, through careful observation, to get to know team members below you with regard to their personality, style, and skill level. When personality conflicts can be prevented (or minimized), each team can better focus on its common purpose, specific performance goals, commitment to the team process, and mutual accountability.

➤ Develop individual and group Emotional Intelligence (EI aka EQ) profiles. Newly formed teams and existing teams that have not worked together for a long time tend to lack balanced conflict management skills. When conflict arises, they either avoid it or divide against one other in various factions. In both cases, productivity comes to a grinding halt. Requiring all executives to study and understand the basic competencies of EI can solve this serious problem. Those executives will then define and create group behavior norms that encourage the group level expression of these competencies. Their next task is to become the primary change agents within the company.

➤ Teach conflict management skills. Managing conflict is rarely, if ever, an innate skill; it must be learned. Teaching by example, through group presentations and individual mentorship is therefore each executive's number-one job. Successful teams do not appear out of thin air; they must be nurtured, grown, and guided. The very best teams function with a high degree of group and individual self-awareness; they're astute in their own understanding of human emotions—of individuals, the entire team, or other groups with whom they interact. And from this center of sophisticated self-awareness, they're able to regulate, balance, and control what might otherwise be unproductive or outright destructive behavior. (For further details on the development of EI or EQ for individuals and groups, refer to the resources listed at the end of this chapter and at the end of Chapter Seven.)

➤ Provide opportunities for junior executives to cooperate and collaborate rather than compete. Encourage those young executives to:

▲ Participate on committees, boards, roundtable discussions, and interdepartmental programs.

▲ Take on stretch assignments and test roles in pairs or trios to develop skills in teamwork, delegating, relationship-building, and conflict management.

▲ Focus on special problem-solving assignments, such as developing a new solution to a manufacturing bottleneck, reengineering a process, increasing efficiency in the supply chain, or getting to the bottom of customer dissatisfaction. When conflict arises in the process of these assignments, have participants take turns mediating it. In addition to learning valuable new skills, they will gain the respect of fellow colleagues.

After a team has developed a creative, uncommon solution collectively or collaboratively, assess how the participants functioned both individually and as a team. Watch for those who recognize and understand that the purpose of a team assignment is to solve a problem collectively, not to provide a flashy vehicle for a rising corporate star. People who "get" what EQ is all about and are able to utilize that knowledge on a practical level—especially as it applies to group dynamics and conflict resolution—are an organization's most valuable employees (and are certainly worth grooming for potential leadership roles).

Six Steps to Managing Conflict

Healthy conflict is the opposite of the "groupthink"—we go along merrily in "agreement" simply to avoid conflict—that has led to major corporate and political disasters. When conflict is managed in a balanced manner and channeled productively, it results in better decisions and greater organizational agility. The conflict management process outlined in the Harvard Business Review article, "How Management Teams Can Have a Good Fight" (Kathleen M. Eisenhardt, Jean L. Kahwajy, and L.J. Bourgeois; 1997) outlines the following six steps for keeping conflict healthy. By implementing these tactics, you can create a model that, if followed, will produce immediate results and serve as a template for succeeding generations of leaders.

1. Focus on the facts.

The authors' research with dozens of companies over a period of ten years demonstrated a direct link between reliance on facts and low levels of interpersonal conflict. Reliance on data grounds discussions and decision-making in reality – i.e., brings the whole discussion down to earth. It encourages people to focus on issues rather than personalities. The more information, the better. Anchor group discussions and team meetings with plenty of accurate, real-time data, both operational and external. Keep debates focused on substantive issues rather than on opinions, hunches, guesses, and extrapolation.

2. Multiply the alternatives.

When only two choices are available, executives tend to become entrenched on one side or the other, resulting in a group behavior that distorts reality and generally results in poor decisions. Few issues in life or in business fall into the category "either/or" options. On the other hand, when multiple alternatives are on the table, conflict is diffused in three ways. First, it creates room for individuals to express varying degrees of support for different choices and to change their minds as the discussion progresses. Second, it encourages the development of integrative solutions that incorporate components of the various choices. Finally, arriving at a solution in this manner is a fun, creative process rather than an endless power struggle. Everyone shares in the ultimate success.

3. Create common goals.

Team members who work toward a common goal are less likely to see themselves as individual winners or losers. A shared vision discourages individual competition and the blame game, while creating a rallying point for the entire group. In an environment where all team or group members have a shared interest, conflict is much less likely to become personal.

4. Use humor.

Research shows that humor is a defense mechanism people use to protect themselves from work-related stress. It creates a positive mood where people are more optimistic, creative, and forgiving. Creating a fun environment with shared social activities, trivial pursuits, whimsical décor, gags, and even practical jokes can relieve the tension of tough decisions and turn colleagues into friends who can agree to disagree.

5. Balance the power structure.

Autocratic and weak leadership, although quite opposite in nature, tend to create the same results: increased levels of interpersonal conflict. Iron-fisted executives generate friction through verbal aggression and, sometimes, aggressive body language. Weak leaders, on the other hand, unwittingly encourage unhealthy competition among the individuals serving under them (these are the unlucky junior executives who know from repeated experience that they must make key decisions in their leader's stead). The solution is a balanced power structure in which all executives participate in strategic decisions. This creates a sense of fairness among the management team. In a healthy power-sharing culture, senior leaders are recognized as holding the most power, but their direct reports possess substantial authority of their own, particularly in their specific areas of responsibility. Dispersed, yet structured empowerment such as this can quickly transform demoralized executive teams into effective and productive units in a very short time.

6. Seek consensus with qualification and equity.

Reaching complete agreement among all team members is rarely possible, and insisting on it tends to increase conflict and stall decision-making processes. However, research on procedural justice shows that people willingly accept outcomes they dislike if they believe the process by which the outcome was determined was fair. Fair, in this case, means that all concerned parties in the process, provided input and felt their influence had an impact on other participants during the undertaking. Based on these findings, the authors recommend a two-step process of reaching "consensus with qualification." First, executives should discuss an issue and try to reach consensus. When such consensus is reached, the decision is final. Second, if consensus remains elusive, the most senior executive makes the decision with input from everyone else. It's a fast, fair, and equitable process.

The Greater Good

Managing conflict in organizations is, in many ways, not unlike the challenges sports coaches face in their efforts to turn youth from tough, inner-city environments into team players. Serving as coach, mentor, teacher, and friend, they succeed in channeling aggression and passion for sports toward the greater good of the team. Their players become not only superstar athletes, but also even better, more effective people in their personal lives. One such coach is John Wooden, the legendary UCLA basketball coach and author of Wooden on Leadership: How to Create a Winning Organization (McGraw-Hill, 2005). Wooden led by example, but also by the force of his convictions. His mission was to ensure that, regardless of the final score, his players always made the utmost effort and performed to the best of their abilities. Among his rules were: "Never score without acknowledging a teammate." "Treat your opponent with respect." "Earn the right to be proud and confident." "It takes 10 hands to score a basket."

The willingness to tackle tough issues, while treating others respectfully, is a key indicator of successful conflict management. When those qualities are enhanced by the willingness to be wrong, to be vulnerable, and to both give and receive feedback, magic often happens. The impossible suddenly becomes imaginable, and the improbable becomes reality. When consensus cannot be reached, those who disagree are not losers. As they agree to go along on the chosen path for the sake of the team, they share in its success.

Case Study: Constructive Conflict?

A marketing executive in the entertainment industry was referred to me for coaching because he was considered too direct and always seemed to be "looking for a fight." We began by discussing his background, during which an important insight into his conflict-management issues emerged. It turned out he had recently been promoted to his position in the United States after having achieved great success in highly visible public relations and marketing positions (with the same company) in a variety of overseas locations.

His description of a typical business meeting in Paris clarified things perfectly. He and his colleagues would meet in a smoky hotel basement room, hashing out difficult marketing issues for up to eight hours at a crack. Sooner or later, patience would wear thin and tempers began to flash. Yelling, name-calling, banging of water glasses, leaping from one's chair, and stomping about were commonplace behaviors. But at the end of the meeting, someone would announce, "Time for dinner!" At this point, everyone adjourned to the restaurant arm in arm, where they would eat, drink, and socialize like the best of friends. The following day, back in the basement, they were at it again like mortal enemies.

Obviously, my coachee's overseas colleagues understood the importance and constructive purpose of conflict. Despite the unruliness of their boiler-room brouhaha, these executives obviously didn't take any of the name-calling, posturing, or other shenanigans personally. Without question, work was accomplished and intelligent decisions emerged from their sessions. But in the United States, executives are much more thin-skinned, constrained, and image-conscious. They tend to shy away from offending others (and from being hurt themselves, poor babies), all of which can subvert and hamper an organization's ability to solve problems collaboratively. Undoubtedly, examples of conflict management from different cultures can provide fascinating and useful insight into any number of business and human-behavior topics. However, the conflict-management lesson my coachee most needed to learn was a very simple one: when in Rome, try to do as the Romans do.

Additional Resources

Boosting Your Team's Emotional Intelligence—For Maximum Performance, Harvard Business Review, www.harvardbusiness.org, Product No. 617X, 2001 (a collection of three articles: *What Makes a Leader?* by Daniel Goleman; *Building Emotional Intelligence in Groups* by Vanessa Urch Druskat and Steven B. Wolff; and *The Discipline of Teams* by Jon R. Katzenbach and Douglas K. Smith).

How Management Teams Can Have a Good Fight by Kathleen M. Eisenhardt, Jean L. Kahwajy, and L.J. Bourgeois, Harvard Business Review, www.harvardbusiness.org, Product No. 97402, 1997.

Wooden on Leadership: How to Create a Winning Organization by John Wooden, McGraw-Hill, 2005.

CHAPTER FIVE
BUILDING RELATIONSHIPS— FOR REAL

He who burns his bridges better be a damn good swimmer.
— Harvey Mackay

Personal relationships are the foundation of a leader's ability to motivate and influence others, obtain resources, and successfully navigate often treacherous corporate waters. Pretty important stuff, right? Then why are most executives unaware of its importance, and why do so many fail to get the most out of their person-to-person relationships? Those questions will be answered in this chapter, along with suggestions for optimizing your ability to nurture and sustain a thriving network that's constructed one human connection at a time, and strategies for passing along this important knowledge to those you coach and develop.

Building relationships is a critical yet sadly neglected skill for talent at all levels in an organization. The truth is that healthy, balanced relationships are at the very heart of an individual's sense of well-being and happiness in life and, arguably, they have a powerful impact on one's level of success—or lack thereof. Human beings are social creatures by nature—no news there! We're hard-wired to function most effectively in the context of an interdependent, vibrant network of individuals, either diverse in their makeup or just like us. When people are confident in their relationships, they tend to be more effective in their various roles, whether at work, at play, or at home. Even seemingly insurmountable problems can be overcome by reaching out to others for help, assurances, and resources—provided one has established good relationships beforehand that one can rely on.

Consequently, on many levels, this may be the book's most important chapter. In it, the discussion centers on how best to coach your team members to develop and nurture relationships with their peers, direct reports, superiors, and other stakeholders. The reality is no one truly ever masters this mysterious subject completely; however, at least striving for improvement sends out the right signal to those around us. There are always new insights to be gained and new skills to achieve, but this chapter contains many rewarding insights and pointers as well as the important benefits that come from utilizing them.

The Importance of Peer-to-Peer Relationships

Senior executives often neglect recognizing high-potential people at the lower levels as part of a future leadership team. Instead, these people are often seen as individual and separate entities, each on their own track of growth and individual path. This tends to create a workplace environment teeming with misdirected competitiveness, a very pervasive and destructive behavioral pattern. In such a corporate culture, people in the lower ranks erroneously view their peers as the competition. They can waste an enormous amount of time and energy striving against peers and others for the attention of their superiors. This, of course, distracts them from the true competition, namely, their counterparts in other companies. As these antagonistic, paranoid, and stressed-out individuals advance in the organization, they bring their skewed perceptions into the senior executive levels. Looking around, they see opponents instead of teammates, and their behavior, in turn, reflects this warped and unhealthy view. In extreme cases, it can become the dominant "reality" of the entire executive team. Trust me, you don't want to allow this type of environment to exist! Effective leadership simply cannot thrive in a culture of mistrust and fierce competitiveness.

Young executives usually manage up very well and believe it to be their ticket to success. Although being on good terms with the boss is obviously vital, high-quality relationships with peers and subordinates are equally, if not more important. Subordinates can, through the quality of their work, make a manager look good or bad. One's peers are similarly powerful; they can obstruct, support, or smooth the way for an emerging talent they can count on and trust.

Find a balance between "managing up, down, and across" is one key to success. It's not easy, though, and it takes practice. Here are some simple steps that can help the people you coach to learn how to build more effective relationships. As your coachees begin to put these steps into practice, be sure to follow up with consistent feedback as described in Chapter Two.

Practice tips for a coachee (and coach!) who needs to enhance confidence and trust, or demonstrate his or her respect for others:

➤ Interact openly and directly with people. Show consistency between words and actions in daily communications.

➤ Admit mistakes. Surprise others with candor and the willingness to make amends.

➤ Give honest answers to questions and challenges. If unable to provide a complete answer, state the reasons why and strive to satisfy the questioner by dealing with those areas you can address.

➤ Take time to think answers through before responding; some people mistrust quick answers.

➤ Keep others as fully informed as possible. Be willing to give them more information than they may actually require.

➤ As you work to improve in these areas, seek feedback from others regarding your openness, honesty, and trustworthiness.

Practice tips for a coachee who is considered unapproachable:

➤ Be willing to investigate the behaviors that create an impression of un-approachability. Ask for feedback from others you know and trust. Make appropriate changes based on this analysis, such as increasing your visibility to and with others. Take an interest in their concerns and problems. Try to spend some time with everyone instead of just one's favorites.

➤ If you are perceived as being cold, impersonal, or overly analytical, make a conscious effort to smile, reach out to people, and engage in friendly small talk. Try sharing some personal information occasionally, and express appreciation of others.

➤ Schedule regular blocks of time for "open door" discussions in which employee concerns can be aired in a more casual, informal manner. Be careful not to schedule other events at these times. Listen intently, and respond non-defensively if some comments hit uncomfortably close to home. These dialogues can be powerful learning opportunities provided you stay calm and don't take things personally.

Practice tips for a coachee who needs to enhance peer relationships:

Emerging leaders need to learn how to cooperate and collaborate with peers rather than to compete with them. It takes practice. Young, ambitious executives often don't realize that their peers (whom they're vying against for the boss's attention) may become their fellow junior executives in a few short years. Instruct hyper-competitive coachees to take the following steps to enhance peer relationships:

➤ Get to know your peers on a personal level. Ask others about accomplishments they're proud of, work-related issues they find challenging, and what new challenges they dream of undertaking.

➤ Encourage collaboration among peers in the development of business initiatives. Explain your thoughts to them and inquire about theirs. Be tentative when stating opinions. Allow peers adequate space so they'll feel comfortable and invested in the collaborative effort. Focus on common goals, priorities, and problems. Invite criticism of ideas. Seek to understand other's wants and needs, and where able, provide help. Finally, develop sensitivity to others' nonverbal cues. The reward is an increased level of buy-in from all collaborators.

➤ Informally ask peers for specific feedback regarding how to improve your working relationship with them. To solicit their feedback:

🔺 Arrange a one-on-one informal meeting with each peer to discuss your working relationship. Don't hold the meeting in either individual's office. Meet, instead, in "neutral territory"— a conference room, cafeteria, or the like.

🔺 Ask peers for specific suggestions on how to improve your working relationship. Focus on listening rather than talking, and respond in an open, honest way. Thank them as they share the insights even if you don't entirely agree with them.

🔺 Invite an objective third party into the meeting if the subjects or the information shared might potentially be difficult to process objectively.

➤ Don't promise more than can be delivered, and don't expect too much from any one meeting! Consistent follow-through is the key to improving relationships and changing peers' perceptions.

Practice tips for a coachee who needs to develop style flexibility or "people skills":
Coachees who need to improve their general social skills or diversify their communication styles will benefit from the following steps:

➤ When managing up, use a crisp communication style for maximum effectiveness. Convey one or two ideas at most. When dealing with the boss, advance preparation before meetings will improve your ability to be concise and succinct. Spend a little time getting centered before beginning, and then clearly articulate the goals, objectives, progress, or concerns. Stay focused, but flexible, and stay attentive to the audience for cues, subtle or otherwise, indicating their desire to ask questions or raise concerns. Take time, when necessary, to address those concerns. Don't simply do "data dumps"—sensitize yourself to the room and keep internally measuring the audience reaction to tailor your message, pace, and volume to ensure you are not losing people.

➤ When reporting to senior management, use a mile-high overview to start with. Outline the topic in broad strokes, before getting to specifics. Weave in phrases such as "I think...", "We recommend...", "A big concern for us is..." as a way to demonstrate confidence and strong knowledge in the topic you are covering.

➤ Speaking to subordinates or peers calls for a more relaxed style. If this is difficult, try visualizing oneself among good friends in an informal setting. When appropriate, loosen up and talk to people as if you were at a picnic. However, when authority is needed, be direct, clear, and frank—but not dictatorial. Avoid speaking too fast or relying on greater intensity and volume to get your points across. Clarity of expression and conciseness of thought are the best tools for enhancing an audience's comprehension of one's message.

Practice tips for a coachee who needs to develop better listening skills:

Active listening is a critical executive skill when it comes to leading others. Here are some simple tips to improve a coachee's listening skills:

➤ **Paraphrase.** Repeat back in your own words what the speaker just said. This has the dual benefit of keeping you tuned in and communicating to the speaker that their message is getting through. Example: "If I understand you correctly, you're saying you think it would be helpful if we were to add people with different backgrounds to the team." Be careful, however, not to overuse this technique or you will be viewed as "a parrot" and someone who is exercising redundancy rather than someone simply striving for a deeper understanding of the topic being presented.

➤ **Ask questions.** A good question is one that seeks to clarify what's just been said rather than to "lead" the discussion in another direction. Questions that seek a more precise understanding of a topic actually benefit both the audience and the speaker. For example: "What kinds of skills do you think we're currently missing and need to augment on the team?"

➤ **Reflect feelings.** Always try to consider the speaker's message in a broader emotional context. How do they feel about it? How emotionally invested are they in the topic? This requires good EQ (Emotional Intelligence) skills and involves deciphering the meaning and intent behind the speaker's actual words. For example: "It sounds as if you're pretty frustrated with not having the resources needed to move the project forward."

➤ **Bridge ideas.** Once a message has been clearly articulated (and comprehended by the group), begin linking new ideas to it. For example: "I can't blame you for feeling as you do. In fact, I think that you've identified much of what has been missing on the project team. My only concern about bringing new people onto the team is being able to bring them up to speed in sufficient time to meet the target date for completion. Do you have any thoughts on how we might approach that?"

Process for Building Networks

Most managers and junior executives in organizations reach their positions because they were very good at what they used to do. Many engineers, planners, problem solvers, and others are promoted to senior leadership positions based on their outstanding performance in those previous roles. And that's where problems often begin in their new roles. Being an effective executive depends primarily upon leadership skills, not technical skills per se, and that means accomplishing work through other people. Human relationships—specifically, one's ability to navigate and thrive within this complex realm —form the very foundation of effective leadership.

Technical experts (engineers, designers, medical professionals, finance people, etc.) who have been promoted to executive positions often encounter serious problems in their ability to lead others. It's easy to understand why: their old career skills, which were technical in nature, are of little help when it comes to understanding, motivating, and leading people; people are not problems to solve, they are "human resources" to be led and directed. Many of these new executives flounder and eventually fail in their new positions because they simply weren't properly tutored in the basics of "Leadership 101."

Three dynamics are common among these ill-prepared executives. First and foremost, they typically lack mentors who can help them in their new roles. Having a mentor or advocate who proactively grows and develops an emerging leader can add great value to that person's development in multiple dimensions. Not only will the emerging leader benefit from the general wisdom that an effective leader can share (and model!), but the emerging leader can also experience how, from a non-technical position, the leader can lead.

Here's an example. A client of mine, a global aerospace company, had a VP Audit position open up. It seemed natural for a junior, but seasoned auditor from the current team to fill that leadership role, but senior leadership opted not to follow that path. Although there were several highly skilled auditors, it was clear that while being skilled technically, none had demonstrated any signs of leadership ability. Oddly, an up-and-comer from Legal was brought in. Although she was more than anxious to take the helm, I reminded her that technical expertise was not what the department needed. It was leadership they needed and that's where she had to focus, and she did. There were skeptics, of course, both inside and outside the department, but in a matter of a few short months, she clearly demonstrated the skill to lead while they, the auditors, audited! Fortunately for the new executive, she had a good mentor, a coach, and the will to succeed. Now she, too, knows why it's important today, more than ever, to do the one thing her predecessor had not done—build a bench of strong, talented leaders within the organization.

Second, when faced with frustration in their attempts to lead other people, many fall back into old (formerly successful) habits. Instead of seeing the bigger picture and delegating tasks to their subordinates, they roll up their sleeves, micromanage like crazy, and try to solve every problem themselves. It does not work and although it's an addiction to be broken, it's a tough row to hoe for many. Third is a dynamic known as "Waving the White Flag from a Fetal Position." This refers to leaders who totally give up, keep to themselves, and hide in their offices. In businesses with a very social work environment (the entertainment industry, for example), this kind of behavior can be a very fast career-breaker. Managers or executives who don't socialize with peers are often viewed as uptight or unsocial. Often they become demoralized and miserable in their new positions and will find it downright impossible to meet any of their assigned objectives, let alone move up in the organization.

Both groups (managers and executives) desperately need to learn the basics of building good relationships at every level. The good news is that any coachee, no matter how introverted or socially uncomfortable, can follow a simple process and build a wide-ranging, effective network. Here are some simple, yet effective ways you can help them:

Step 1: Construct a "social hit list."

Help them assemble a list of people, at various levels in the organization, with whom they need more visibility and connection. Help them understand that to be successful in this endeavor they must first create an internal commitment to interact more effectively with peers and subordinates. Once that decision has been made, they need to follow up by actually writing down the names of specific people who either deserve or require more executive "face time" with them.

Step 2: Divide and conquer. Put people on the list into coffee, lunch, and dinner groups.

People with whom there is a slight discomfort, for whatever reason, go into the "Coffee Group"—these are short and sweet meetings with a clear purpose, such as discussing an upcoming project in a somewhat informal setting. Having coffee with someone is very safe; if things get uncomfortable, one can simply drink up, cordially end the conversation, and leave. (How simple is that?)

The "Lunch Group" consists of people with whom the coachee is more comfortable. These are the folks one would enjoy eating lunch with and talking to in a more in-depth way. The meeting is still somewhat short in duration but leaves additional room for social interaction while getting business done in an informal, more comfortable setting.

The "Dinner Group" is reserved for those the coachee already knows, likes, and wants to get to know even better. This level of interaction will help immensely in deepening connections in a safe environment.

Ideally, the coachee should create a list of approximately twelve people distributed over the three groups. For each individual, they need to make note of a specific piece of business to discuss. The item can relate to the other person directly or indirectly. Think of it as a "getting to know you" opportunity, an ice-breaking conversation and an olive branch, all rolled into one neat package. Most people will be impressed and probably moved by the thoughtfulness of the gesture.

Where I have successfully coached clients to do this, positive feedback about their outreach "raged like wildfire," and people remarked about "the change" they had seen—all from this simple gesture. If the coachee is very uncomfortable or has difficulty reaching out to certain people, he or she can engage a third party to facilitate a three-way meeting. A mutually familiar person can ease the tension considerably and make the situation both more enjoyable and productive.

Here's an example. "Roxanne" is a senior female executive in finance at a division of an entertainment industry giant. Described as "bookish" and "shy," as part of building her network, she decided to meet "Andrea," a well-seasoned junior female executive at Corporate Center who was about the same age. Both were quite uncomfortable with the idea of meeting and asked me to attend. I started off the meeting by asking Roxanne a question about her interests outside of work, which she answered enthusiastically. I then asked Andrea the same question. At one point during Andrea's response, Roxanne chimed in with a comment, and within minutes, they were engaged in a spontaneous and animated discussion. My job complete, I sat back and, for the next hour, thoroughly enjoyed listening to their conversation and musing on the benefits and simple joys that can be found in human relationships. At one point they "realized" that I was still sitting there and we all chuckled at that fact and that they had become fast friends. Andrea then became our "ambassador" and word spread fast about Roxanne and how "approachable" she was and what a joy to work with. Mission accomplished!

Step 3: The art of scheduling meetings—just do it!

Time to move from theory and preparation into action. Have the coachee take the list in hand and begin making telephone calls to schedule breakfast, lunch, and dinner meetings. Even better than phone calls, are in-person invitations when possible. That means walk over to the next aisle, office, or the other side of the building—it's a great way to impress the other person and get a little bit of exercise at the same time. E-mailing and texting are not allowed—or at least not preferred! It's too impersonal for person-to-person matters like these. Here are some great conversation starters to get you going:

➤ "It's been a while since we chatted, and I have something on my radar screen that doesn't involve you directly, but it's going to affect you down the road. I'd love to grab a cup of coffee with you and give you a heads-up. Would next Tuesday work for you?"

➤ "Something is coming up in the next quarter that's going to involve you and your team. I'd love to get a head start with you, just to talk about it one-on-one with no commitment. Can we grab lunch later this week?"

> ➤ "Next quarter has projects on the table that I am managing and before we launch, I'd love to have your input. Can we schedule a dinner later this month? I'd hate to rush the discussion over just coffee or a chat."

Step 4: Engineer a relaxed first meeting.

The goal is to meet people in a less formal situation where each person can feel relaxed. It's a great opportunity to present a different view of oneself, namely, as a living, breathing human being, not just the manager who reports the numbers at the monthly meeting. The coachee should start off with a bit of small talk and express interest in the other person. He or she should then communicate awareness of the other person's job-related efforts and explain how they're going to be affected by upcoming events or decisions. Bringing a proposal or bulleted notes that lay out the relevant details is a good tactic. Then— and this is very important—have the coachee invite the other person's insights regarding those plans and explain that any feedback will be taken seriously and may, in fact, result in modifications to the forthcoming decisions. The coachee should encourage comments by asking, "So, what do you think?", "How does this affect you?", or "How can I work with you more closely?" At this point, it's critical to practice good listening skills. Warn the coachee not to lecture! Falling into that trap can ruin a potentially very productive meeting.

Step 5: Maintain and grow the relationship.

Relationships are like a garden, they grow best when tended to carefully and diligently, as the old adage goes. It's fun to plant the seeds, but the real work comes later: pulling weeds, watering and, of course, harvesting when the time is right. Nurturing a relationship involves growing a broad and deep network from which one can draw strength, ideas, and resources. Just as importantly, it's also about giving back those same gifts when others need assistance. Commitment, time, and patience are essential ingredients in building relationships. Too many coachees jump in with both feet on those initial coffee, lunch, and dinner dates, but fail to follow up with adequate care over the long term. Discipline and consistency are the watchwords. Good intentions are of little value; action and follow-through are what really count. Without relationships, people work in a vacuum. Healthy and thriving relationships that reach across departments and throughout organizational and leadership levels, on the other hand, provide the currency with which one barters for needed resources, money, time, and manpower. Good relationships benefit everyone. Coachees should make a point of introducing people above or below them to their network of friends and associates, and talk up their talents and abilities. It's not only the polite thing to do—it's one's duty. (Executives who aren't mentors aren't real leaders). When promotion opportunities arise, those lucky subordinates, and others, will benefit from already being widely known. The best way to teach people how to build relationships is to demonstrate it, every day. Involve them in the process. It's contagious! Direct reports and peers will gradually gain confidence, step up, and begin building great workplace relationships for themselves. Watching this process blossom in a coachee is as good as it gets. This is where many executives find the greatest sense of accomplishment—and joy —in their careers.

Is It Working?

How can a coachee (or a coach, for that matter) tell if relationship-building initiatives are working? The soft measure of improved relationships is determined by how coachees are treated by other people. Are they respected and spoken well of by their peers and subordinates? Those are critically important indications to watch for, in addition to the following:

> Do people greet the coachee warmly?

> Is the coachee treated with genuine respect (as opposed to fear-motivated flattery)?

> Do other people speak well of the coachee to their associates, friends, and peers?

➤ What are they likely to say after the coachee leaves the room? (Otherwise known as the "fly on the wall" test.)

A more clear-cut measure of success becomes evident when a coachee is up against the wall and in need of support. Do others spontaneously step up and deliver? Do they share resources and time to help the coachee out of a tight spot? If so, then the coachee has been successful in building relationships based on a mutual willingness to sacrifice and offer assistance to each other. This is the acid test! Do other people willingly champion a coachee's cause with a committee or team of seniors? When the chips are down, are people there for the coachee, and does the coachee support others when the roles are reversed? True success for any executive is built on a foundation of accomplishments of the people below and across organizations. It must be earned by one's actions and skills in the complicated realm of human emotions. Emerging leaders who have built good relationships will be rewarded with the solid loyalty and sincere trust of their subordinates and others throughout their careers.

Work Smarter

Building good relationships is the best way to work smarter. Other skills such as outstanding problem-solving expertise, successful program management, widget-designing wizardry, or the ability to land a big client are obviously vital qualities. But a truly distinguishing trait comes from the success of establishing and nurturing good relationships. That means broadening one's network at multiple levels and across business lines. It requires taking some risks, getting out of the office, thinking about other people's welfare, and not single-mindedly tooting one's own horn. In short, it means being the kind of person who acts like a true team player in both good times and when the chips are down. Now there's a legacy to build!

Additional Resources

How Leaders Create and Use Networks by Herminia Ibarra and Mark Hunter, Harvard Business Review, www.harvardbusiness.org, Product No. R0701C, 2007.

Results Through Relationships: Building Trust, Performance, and Profit Through People by Joe Takash, Wiley, 2008.

Breakthrough Networking: Building Relationships That Last by Lillian D. Bjorseth, Duoforce Enterprises, Inc., 2009.

CHAPTER SIX
MASTERING THE ART OF MOTIVATION

What makes life dreary is the want of a motive.

— George Eliot

Most leaders know that motivating employees is important, but only a few know how to do it effectively. Even fewer make time for it. One reason for this lapse may be the widespread misunderstanding of what, precisely, motivates people. Contrary to popular belief, money is not among the top workplace motivators. In fact, financial incentives are nowhere near the top of the list. Frederick Herzberg, whose classic work on motivation in the 1950s and 1960s, demonstrated that people are primarily motivated by interesting and challenging work, along with increasing levels of responsibility. These intrinsic factors, Herzberg said, answer people's deep-seated need for growth and achievement. But today, most organizations still rely on compensation, fringe benefits, and incentive packages, which tend to drive people to perform only so as long as it takes to win that next raise or promotion.

Motivation appears to be one of those elusive qualities that is very difficult to both teach and measure. Difficult, yes, but far from impossible! A related concept, equally challenging to impart or track, is "morale," the emotional underpinning of motivation. High morale is the good "vibe" one finds in an environment of exceptionally enthusiastic and passionate people.

This chapter provides some simple tools you can use to keep people highly energized and motivated on a proactive and consistent basis. You will discover what motivates people, how to boost morale, and improve both the efficiency and productivity of employees at all levels. You will also learn how to transfer your motivating skills to direct reports so they, in turn, can jump-start and maintain high motivation levels within their team.

How Motivated Is Your Organization?

To assess an organization's "motivational intelligence," begin by considering the following questions:

1. Is morale low? Are people pessimistic despite your best efforts to promote a positive attitude? Do employees grumble frequently? Do you see a pattern of people calling in "sick" or barely managing to drag themselves in on Monday mornings?

2. Is productivity either flat or dropping off, despite rising salaries, more time off, better benefits, and bonuses?

3. Do people exhibit a "bunker" mentality? Do they simply hunker down to get the work done, demonstrating poor (or non-existent) communication techniques and a pronounced lack of enthusiasm?

4. Do many obviously talented individuals perform at subpar levels?

5. Do people climb over each other in their desire to be the star or win a big promotion?

If the answer is "yes" to any of these questions, motivation is probably lacking. If the answers were "no," that's a good sign, but there is always room for improvement. Consider the following questions to gain some insight regarding where improvements might be appropriate:

1. Are people genuinely enthusiastic, optimistic, and cheerful? Are they passionate about their roles and activities, eager to work with fellow team members, and wholeheartedly engaged in their assigned projects?

2. Does communication flow freely among departments? Do people share information and help one another get the job done?

3. When people encounter problems completing a task, do they seek help from the executives to whom they report?

4. Is employee turnover low?

5. Does the corporate environment encourage creativity and innovation?

If you answered "yes" to all of these questions, congratulations and high fives all around! If, on the other hand, some "no" responses surfaced, keep reading, and pay particular attention to the topic areas that prompted those problematic answers. They will provide direction and clues for the motivation-related changes required to move a company and its people from "good" to "great."

Assessing Individual Motivation: The Skill/Will Matrix

Having gained a general sense—a non-scientific but nonetheless accurate "assessment" of the motivation level of your organization—the next step is to assess motivation person by person. We'll start with the Skill/Will Matrix. It's an excellent way to objectively measure and help employees understand their skill and motivation levels. It involves an assessment that compares how employees view their performance and motivation levels against how their bosses rate them. This type of informal "gap analysis" serves as a basis for measuring overall motivation levels for individuals and teams. (The Skill/Will Matrix was introduced by Max Landsberg in *The Tao of Coaching: Boost Your Effectiveness at Work by Inspiring and Developing Those Around You* (Profile Books, 2009. It may ultimately be derived from the 1970s Hersey-Blanchard situational leadership theory developed by Paul Hersey, author of Situational Leader (Center for Leadership Studies, 1992) and Ken Blanchard, a management guru who later coauthored the One Minute Manager series. Hersey and Blanchard argued that the right leadership style depends on the followers' competence and commitment (low competence/high commitment, some competence/low commitment, high competence/variable commitment, high competence/high commitment).

Here's how the matrix works. Draw a simple X/Y axis. Along the left side, write SKILL; along the bottom write MOTIVATION. The point where the two lines converge in the bottom left corner represents zero skill and zero motivation. The top left on the Y axis represents 100 percent skill and the far right on the X axis represents 100 percent motivation. Distribute blank graphs to your direct reports and/or coachees, asking them to rate themselves on a scale from 0 to 100 in terms of their skill level. Have them mark that position on the graph. Then ask them to rate themselves in terms of motivation, and mark that position on the graph. Finally, have everyone draw lines up and across to determine the convergence point of the two scores. Each individual will fall into one of the following four quadrants; each quadrant describes a general area where development efforts need to be focused:

High skill, low motivation	High skill, high motivation
Low skill, low motivation	Low skill, high motivation

For example, individuals rating themselves at 90 percent "skill" and 80 percent "motivation" earn an overall score of 90/80. Their mark should be placed in the upper right-hand quadrant. That's where all the high-performers in an organization should be clustered. Important note: Be certain employees understand that this exercise is only a tool for informal discussion and will not be recorded in the personnel file. This will encourage greater candor of employee self-assessments (hence, higher accuracy) and will dramatically lower any tension, suspicion, and mistrust that might—quite understandably —accompany this exercise.

While employees fill in their graphs, informally rank each individual according to your sense of their overall skill and motivation levels. In most cases, this score will differ from theirs. Next, meet individually with each employee to discuss the gap. Be prepared to revise your scores upward in lieu of what might come to light during such conversations (e.g., an employee's successful completion of significant tasks or professional development activities of which one was previously unaware). Conversely, if your scores for the employee are markedly lower than the employee's self-scores, be prepared to create a developmental plan to increase skill and/or motivation levels.

Understanding What Motivates People

The biggest mistake leaders make in this area is assuming that one size fits all. Some throw money at employees, believing it provides motivation, while others crack the whip. In reality, the variety of effective motivational tools is as diverse as today's workforce. Monetary rewards, for example, often work well for sales staff that are stimulated by ever-increasing bonuses and special rewards tied to increased sales numbers. But don't count on financial incentives to motivate everyone.

An extensive body of research reaffirms that extrinsic rewards often inspire people temporarily, but they do not create lasting motivation (the kind that genuinely transforms organizations). Those short-term rewards include spiraling wage structures, bonuses, titles, perks, time off, and incentive management systems tied directly to team and individual performances.

Another mistake when it comes to motivational practices involves forcing employees to compete for rewards. This approach tends to erode teamwork and encourages employees to view each other as the competition rather than focusing on beating the real competition—other companies in your market. In this case, the results are often a "life-is-a-jungle" corporate culture in which employees trample over each other in their race for individual gain, rather than striving for organizational successes.

On the other hand, intrinsic rewards are the best form of motivating employees for the long-term. People have a deep need for stimulating work. In fact, most people love to work. This is a profound concept not understood by most executives, to the great loss of the business world. But here's an equally important insight: that work must be interesting (stimulating and challenging) and allow people to be surrounded by like-minded coworkers. They want challenges that offer opportunities for achievement, opportunities for personal and professional growth, and the joy of leading (or working collaboratively on a team) with other motivated individuals. Motivating means energizing people and satisfying these and other intrinsic needs. Pushing people with extrinsic "bribes" or control mechanisms won't provide the juice needed to transform a demoralized organization into a high-performing one. Most people resent being controlled; they fervently desire control over their own destiny. As an expert in the field, Herzberg distinguishes two types of basic human needs. One stems from mankind's animal nature and includes the fundamental requirements for food, shelter, safety, and security. The other need arises out of unique human characteristics. This includes, for example, the desire to achieve constructive goals and to experience the accompanying psychological growth. When an autocratic boss cracks the whip, people's animal needs are threatened, and, without question, they get busy (or, in most cases, look really busy). But true motivation is absent. In such toxic environments, the most promising talent jumps ship (or at least starts looking), while a few remaining people tend to stay out of fear or because they hope their wagon is hitched to a star (probably a poor bet). One thing, however, is certain: the road ahead will be a rough and rocky one!

Even more astonishing is this fact: employees who expect a reward for completing a task typically underperform compared to those who expect no reward. This turns a great deal of modern business practices upside down, doesn't it? At the executive level, studies reveal minimal or even negative correlations between pay and performance, as measured by corporate profitability and other criteria ("Incentive Plans Cannot Work" by Alfie Kohn, Harvard Business Review, 2002). In short, pay-for-performance only gains temporary compliance (at best). It changes behavior in the short term, but cannot create enduring commitment or meaningful organizational transformation.

It's important to understand that everyone possesses inherent motivation—yes, everyone. People are simply hard-wired to be enthusiastic about something, although it may be dormant within them or not easily noticed by an outside observer. Or, worst-case scenario, what motivates them is not what they do under your employ—and that is a whole different conversation. Therefore, it shouldn't come as any surprise that individuals who appear totally unmotivated at work, often excel in other pursuits (e.g., sports, hobbies, or family and community activities). The key is to discover what motivates every individual and find a way to channel that innate drive for excellence into his or her workplace roles. Bottom line: motivation has to come from within each person; it cannot be imposed from the outside. But it can be nurtured!

Eleven Steps to Motivating People

Once you understand what really motivates people, a path can be charted to a new type of organizational culture, namely, an environment where energized, enthusiastic employees can excel for the right reasons. Now is the right time to do away with bribes and coercion! Here are eleven innovative ways to genuinely motivate people to achieve their optimal levels of job-related performance and satisfaction (keeping in mind that happy employees are generally productive ones):

1.   Set the bar higher. Many people are motivated by a challenge. What better way to improve productivity than by helping individuals stretch their wings with new assignments and challenges? The more they contribute, the more highly motivated they become.

2.   Give people room to shine as individuals. Increase someone's responsibility by letting him or her complete an entire process rather than just a piece of it.

3.   Find the right hand for each glove. Assign specialized tasks to individuals who have a particular interest or talent. Allow them to become resident experts and follow up by appointing them to advisory positions within specific teams or departments. Then watch the corporate skies light up with a whole new constellation of bright stars!

4.   Recognize more experienced individuals' expertise by giving them the opportunity to coach or mentor a novice. Few roles are more rewarding than this one, especially for more senior execu-

tives. It's tragic, the degree to which corporate America fails to capitalize on its population of wise elders within (and recently retired from) the business world.

5. Mix it up and get out of the office! Spend time among the troops every day. "Manage by walking around," so to speak, to create visibility and connection to your people and what they are doing. Ask what they need to achieve their goals and then provide the requested support. Be kind and thoughtful. Don't underestimate the impact of simple things such as sponsoring team lunches or bringing in donuts (I'm just not a bagel guy) or pizza—not as a bribe—but rather as an opportunity for informal fellowship with your people. Keep it light and have some fun!

6. Create an unambiguous vision of a positive, vibrant, and mutually supportive work environment. Most people like helping each other and working together. Envision and articulate a healthy, trusting culture with open communication channels where people support each other and where competitiveness is directed at their counterparts in other companies. Turn it into a company-wide conversation.

7. Set a good example. That old saying from the 1970s, "Your attitude determines your altitude," remains true today. Motivating others comes easily to leaders who are naturally and genuinely motivated, optimistic, and passionate about their work. Executives who grumble or trash the boss, other teams, peers, and direct reports set a harmful example that their subordinates will surely emulate either overtly or covertly. The inevitable result is a decline in both morale and motivation (along with increased alienation and outright paranoia). Require every executive and manager to "walk the talk" of the company's vision. This commitment to a new organizational culture must spill over into the senior management team's personal lives, too. Today's employees are extraordinarily savvy—they intensely scrutinize how their bosses work, live, and play. Lasting change in this regard must originate from the top. A

word of caution: avoid false optimism, as it will only lead others to question one's sincerity (and sanity!) Remember that sincere, effective leaders are realists, too.

8. Show your human side. If someone is unmotivated, care enough to discover why. Have an informal, confidential conversation and find out what really ails them. Are they feeling trapped, no longer finding the work satisfying? Demoralized because the budget has been cut? Working sixty hours a week and burned out? Not feeling challenged? Has good work gone unrecognized? Really listen to their answers, and then get busy unblocking barriers at work that hinder motivation. For example, if a problem stems from personal or family challenges, refer the person to a counseling professional. Assure them that their candor about personal matters such as these will be rewarded with strict confidentiality on your part.

9. Don't be afraid to fail. For example, try loosening controls over certain individuals who complain they are held back by excessively rigid constraints. Rely instead on their innate sense of accountability (in other words, trust them to do the right thing!). Let them know exactly what and why this is being done. Then watch and measure the results. If it doesn't work, try something different.

10. Rethink performance management according to what really motivates people. Provide coaching, feedback, and role modeling to help people grow personally and professionally. Traditional measures of success based on quantification (i.e., less time spent on customer service calls, bigger accounts brought in, and the like) do not motivate people—they make them feel manipulated and driven. Instead, design reward systems that stretch and motivate people as individuals while advancing company goals.

11. Create "reflective structures." In the 1990s, leadership guru Warren Bennis found that leaders who built into their lives what he called "reflective structures"—time and space for self-examina-

tion—stayed in touch with what was important to them. Reflective structures come in a wide variety of forms and can range from spiritual practices to physical exercise. When individuals are in touch with what really matters to them, they are more open about their motivations and more easily motivated by intrinsic means.

The greatest leaders are great motivators. They built their success not on the backs of subordinates, but on the foundation created for them by the people who grant them their leadership status. They know how to rally the troops. In the terms of emotional intelligence, these are the highly "socially aware" people who engage others and pull them in. They are charismatic, transparent, and genuine. Fakes and poseurs are quickly seen for who they really are and are not taken seriously or well respected.

Case Study: Creating Followers

When Glaxo Wellcome and SmithKline Beecham merged in 2000, George Morrow, (President and CEO of Glaxo Wellcome) fully intended to retire within five years. Instead, Amgen snapped him up where he now serves as executive vice president of Global Commercial Operations. As he moved from North Carolina to California, a number of his people followed so they could continue to work with him. What a great case study, if you will, that successful professional people were willing to uproot themselves and their families to follow a leader across the country. Here are some of the methods Morrow recommends for creating a base of loyal followers and keeping them motivated:

- Set high standards and give people the resources to achieve them. When Morrow's team members were asked why they followed him, they mentioned his qualities as a benevolent leader who inspires and motivates. Those attributes include caring about his employees while, at the same time, holding them to very high standards. Morrow expects nothing but the best of his people, and gives them everything they need to achieve that high level of excellence. When Morrow was asked why people follow him, his response echoed the same core message: "I know that they will get the job done if I give them the resources they need."

➢ A thorough, effective performance management process. Amgen uses 360 Degree evaluations, gap analysis, a company-wide employee opinion survey, effective feedback, coaching, and mentoring. "Our top district managers and sales representatives are the product of great mentoring and coaching," says Morrow. "They are four, five or even ten times more productive than others."

➢ Develop emotional intelligence (EI/EQ). Morrow believes it's a leader's responsibility to balance work functions while focusing on the emotional relationships within the organization's teams. A critical tool in this effort is emotional intelligence. "When employees lack in EQ, they usually elevate conflict to a level where it becomes an internal contest," he says. "This is a drag on the system and provides the competition with an advantage. These conflicts are destructive for our organization." Emotional intelligence is vital for leaders who want to either jump-start a lackluster organization or to maintain a company's motivation and productivity at the highest levels.

Measuring the ROI of Motivation

Measuring the success (or failure) of efforts to motivate others is not always easy. A "soft" way is to observe the overall morale of an organization. Are people enthusiastic? Are they eager, optimistic, and cheerful? Are they passionate about projects they're engaged in? Do they exhibit a gung-ho attitude in their collaborations with fellow team members and their bosses? These critical soft factors may be unscientific, but are nonetheless important and valid measures. They're obtained simply by paying attention as you move through your daily routine. For harder, more precise measurements, examine productivity levels. Enthusiastic and passionate teams sell more and accomplish more, in less time, with fewer resources than do their less-motivated counterparts. But always remember: in any measure of motivation, it's important to distinguish true motivation from the short-term drive created by financial incentives, promises of promotion, desire for the limelight, accolades, or increased recognition from "higher-ups."

Choose Excellence Over Business as Usual

The vast majority of leaders don't set out to intentionally demotivate their people or consciously set them up for failure. However, that's precisely the result of so many of their misguided attempts at motivation. Ultimately, these leaders fail to serve the best interests of their organizations and themselves. Most of these executives sincerely want to do the right things for their companies and their stockholders. The problem is they don't know what they don't know.

Some executives, on the other hand, do know better. For a variety of reasons, however, they refuse to invest the time and energy needed to effectively motivate their people. Surprisingly enough, they can often muddle through in this fashion for years. Somehow, the work gets done, the company stays afloat, and the leadership, such as it is, remains at the helm. But it begs the following question: what do such leaders really want from their people, their companies, and themselves—maintenance of a lackluster status quo or run-of-the-mill performance instead of stellar achievement? Are they truly happy with mediocrity? Of course not! Deep down, they want what every person desires: the opportunity and resources to do excellent work and to be appreciated for it.

The chief problem of these executives lies in not knowing specifically how to get from here to there. And that's what this chapter is all about. It should be clear by now that if a leader desires organizational and personal excellence, then genuine motivation is the only sure way to achieve it. Start the process by assessing what motivates people in the organization. Determine what really turns them on. Find creative ways of motivating them individually and as team players. Keep in mind that one's ultimate goal is to create an environment in which people feel acknowledged and recognized for their accomplishments, where creativity and innovation are rewarded, and everyone is given challenging goals and the tools to accomplish them. For those leaders who thirst for something better than business as usual, welcome to the adventure of a lifetime!

Additional Resources

The Set-Up-to-Fail Syndrome by Jean-Francois Manzoni and Jean-Louis Barsoux, Harvard Business Review, www.harvardbusiness.org, Product No. 861X, 2002.

How to Motivate Your Problem People by Nigel Nicholson, Harvard Business Review, www.harvardbusiness.org, Product No. 2780, 2003.

One More Time: How Do You Motivate Employees? by Frederick Herzberg, Harvard Business Review, www.harvardbusiness.org, Product No. R0301F, 2003.

Rethinking Rewards by Alfie Kohn, Harvard Business Review, www.harvardbusiness.org, Product No. 93610, 1993.

Why Incentive Plans Cannot Work by Alfie Kohn, Harvard Business Review, www.harvardbusiness.org, Product No. 2799, 2003.

Management by Whose Objectives? by Harry Levinson, Harvard Business Review, www.harvardbusiness.org, Product No. R0301H, 2003.

Primal Leadership: Realizing the Power of Emotional Intelligence by Daniel Goleman, Richard Boyatzis, and Annie McKee, Harvard Business School Press, www.harvardbusiness.org, Product No. 486X, 2002.

Reawakening Your Passion for Work by Richard Boyatzis, Annie McKee, and Daniel Goleman, Harvard Business Review, www.harvardbusiness.org, Product No. 9659, 2002.

The Tao of Coaching: Boost Your effectiveness at Work by Inspiring and Developing Those Around You by Max Landsberg, Profile Books, 2009.

CHAPTER SEVEN
HARNESSING THE POWER
OF INFLUENCE

Honest disagreement is often a good sign of progress

— Mahatma Gandhi

L et's face it: in the context of human relations, the verb "influence" has a bad rap. Ask anyone who hasn't actually read Dale Carnegie's classic work, How to Win Friends and Influence People, what they think the book is about. More than likely, their first guess will be that it's about manipulating people in some way. Well, Carnegie's book is not about that; nor is this chapter. Real influencing—the kind discussed here—is a powerful, constructive leadership tool that furthers rapport, trust, and cooperation for the purpose of garnering resources and support. It's an essential tool and skill of every effective leader. And there's nothing intrinsically dishonest or sneaky about it.

The fact is: manipulation is starkly different from influence. The former is a covert action designed to deceive, stemming from a personal agenda. Think of manipulation as a jackknife kept hidden in someone's back pocket… it's really for nefarious purposes. Influence, on the other hand, is symbolized by the hand extended in friendship, the pat on the back for a job well done, and most importantly, the ability to persuasively unite others in a common cause that advances the greater good. Since the exercise of leadership is concerned with getting things done through others, what skill is more important or useful than being an excellent influencer?

The purpose of this chapter is to increase your efficiency and effectiveness by being a powerful influencer. You'll develop better influencing skills yourself and learn how to transfer those skills to the next generation of leaders.

When Do You Need Influencing Skills?

"Everyone influences all the time, but most people are simply not aware of doing so," says Alan Vengel, author of The Influence Edge: How to Persuade Others to Help You Achieve Your Goals (Berrett-Koehler Publishers, 2001). "Raising awareness of how you use influence and what effect it has on others is the first step to becoming a better influencer. Once you become conscious of approaches that have worked with some people, but not others, you can start targeting your approach to influence."

Top salespeople know the secret of success has little to do with a given product or its price, but rather the salesperson's ability to influence buyers. As such, they continually seek ways to connect with potential buyers—in short, by speaking their language. They channel their influential powers into persuasion, another frequently misunderstood term. Genuine persuasion is not about cajoling or bullying people into something they don't want or don't need. Nor is it about covertly or overtly undermining someone's point of view in order to sell a product or advance your agenda. It means winning someone to your side by utilizing interpersonal skills that build rapport and trust.

Obviously, influencing is not a skill limited to sales and closing deals. "Young people in organizations often believe that doing their job is enough and don't realize that they also need to become savvy about influencing others to 'sell' their ideas, resolve conflict, gain support for initiatives and work with teams," says Vengel. In fact, influencing is an extremely critical leadership skill and a powerful, constructive tool that, used correctly, can help you and others:

➤ Gain resources and support in order to complete projects and achieve objectives.

➤ Build consensus, rapport, and trust to get people on board for a change initiative.

➤ Persuade superiors to assign more challenging projects to under-recognized and under-utilized staffers.

➤ Represent one's team as an ambassador to a superior (or another team), to gain resources or win support.

➤ Create positive exposure for one's department, people or projects, and get others to recognize one's unrecognized contributions and overall value.

➤ Establish common ground and strong bonds between antagonists by convincing them of the wisdom (and long-term benefits) of becoming team players who share a "big picture" view instead of their own individual agendas.

Developing Influencing Skills

Unless you're one of the lucky few for whom influencing comes naturally, acquiring these skills will take practice. Where do you begin? And how do you coach your team members in critical influencing skills?

The first step is to familiarize yourself and become articulate in the language of EI or EQ (Emotional Intelligence). What is EI? And what does it have to do with this discussion of influencing? EI is not a complex model. Its core tenet is that although business is business, it's conducted entirely by people, and people are human beings. They're not machines; nor are they theoretical abstracts or chess pieces that can be moved interchangeably from box to box in an organization chart. We all live, breath, and conduct business in a vibrant, diverse milieu absolutely brimming—and sometimes bursting over—with countless variations of emotion-driven, sometimes quite irrational human behavior.

So, regardless of environment, people are driven by emotions that function like an internal engine. For our purposes in this chapter, EI is not concerned with leaders becoming better able to express their emotions (such as happiness, anger, or frustration). Rather, it's about leaders recognizing and more effectively managing their own emotions as they affect and impact their relationships with others. This latter goal is of particular importance. It requires leaders to continually improve their ability to develop rapport with other people and to be sensitive to their needs and desires. This skill is extremely critical for enlisting cooperation and for moving teams toward desired outcomes. It's a skill you should model for those you lead and grow to be the next generation of leaders.

EI should not be confused with the idea of becoming more "sociable," although some similarities do exist. It's a fine distinction, but one worth making. Social skill, according to Goleman, is "friendliness with a purpose." The importance of social skill extends from interaction with employees, peers, and bosses to customer relationships. People in sales or customer service positions, for example, need excellent social skills in order to anticipate customers' needs so they can meet or exceed them.

EI seeks to go beyond mere social agility, and can only be developed or enhanced through thoughtful, focused leadership development. Don't look to traditional training programs to boost EI, warns Goleman. Instead, EI goals are met only by extended practice, feedback from colleagues, coaching, and the executive's own drive for personal growth. This pursuit is a wonderful place to channel a potential leader's "fire in the belly;" the truth is, they'll need all they can get.

The Four Steps to Effective Influencing

Influencing others is both an art and a science. Breaking it down into four basic steps will take some of the mystery out of it and get you started on the right foot in terms of developing your influencing skills:

Step 1: Build relationships.

People who use intimidation or promises of rewards to win others to their side generally do not build rapport or trust with other people, for a variety of reasons (most having to do with their own personality traits). When it comes to genuine influencing, however, it's absolutely essential to nurture relationships and establish oneself as trustworthy. That means consistently following through on commitments and demonstrating that you truly care about others, from subordinates and superiors to peers. Take the time to meet with people individually. Listen carefully to their concerns and opinions. Ask questions. Seek to understand, not just to be understood.

Make honest, two-way feedback a basis for every dialogue. The most crucial element of this process is to connect with people emotionally. "Feedback is a critical component of training someone in influencing skills," says author Alan Vengel. "Asking people how you come across as an influencer and relationship-builder can be a real eye-opener. Before-and-after feedback is a useful measurement of progress."

People who are successful at building and maintaining relationships walk the talk. They don't go through the motions simply to win support for a specific initiative. They demonstrate trustworthiness, respect, fairness, and personal responsibility in all their interactions. They are "people" people who genuinely care about others. Young executives who find it difficult to build and maintain relationships will require some coaching to increase their emotional intelligence (EI) and social skills. A good place to start is with a homework assignment: ask each executive to read, study and be prepared to discuss Daniel Goleman's work on EI (it's listed in the Additional Resources' section at the end of this chapter).

Step 2: Make your case.
Influencing people to gain support or resources is much easier when it's based on a foundation of good relationships. In such an atmosphere, your credentials and credibility are common knowledge; you're in good standing. So how do you win others over to your cause? To start, present compelling evidence for your position or request, supported by examples and statistics. Highlight the benefits of your proposal and any unique information or special knowledge acquired in your research. Most executives are familiar with presenting a good case.

An equally crucial component of winning support is to focus on emotional impact. You will need excellent communication skills to "read" your audience and adjust your presentation to get your message across. An outstanding tool in this regard is storytelling, one of the oldest and most powerful methods of communication. "Become therefore a mighty craftsman in thy speech, for thereby shalt thou gain in life the victory," says an ancient Egyptian inscription.

A well-chosen story can communicate your strategic goals and priorities to others, while simultaneously making an emotional connection. People have a strong emotional need to belong and contribute, and storytelling can speak powerfully to those deepseated needs. While people may not remember your facts and statistics, they'll nearly always remember a compelling story and the point it made. Bring things full circle by encouraging others to share similar stories; it's an excellent way to get people involved in the process and create additional support for your viewpoint.

Step 3: Build consensus.

Consensus quite literally means "a sharing of the minds." It does not necessarily mean getting others to change their minds and agree with you. In fact, the opposite is quite often true. An effective influencer uses consensus-building to win overall support while allowing others the right to disagree or to hold differing ideas. Consensus-builders always demonstrate high regard and respect for the thoughts, opinions, and judgment of other people. There's no room for autocrats in a consensus-centric organization! The challenge here—and it's a difficult one—is to continually strive to remain open-minded and willing to compromise. Yet conversely, when it's only consensus that we seek, decisions are at risk of never being made! Strive for balance in this approach to reap the full benefits of influence (by including others in the process) and true leadership (making the tough call sometimes, even when it's not fully agreed on).

Let's assume you've successfully won support for your initiative. Time to rest on your laurels and graciously accept the accolades of other people, right? Wrong! Now's the time to get busy.

Honor the help that other people have given you by supporting them, in turn. Influencing is a two-way street. If you treat it as a one-way street, your relationships with people will erode, and then it's back to Step 1.

Now let's consider a less positive outcome: You've given it your best shot, but your breathtaking presentation and astonishing storytelling failed to win people to your position. What now? First, don't force the issue. Instead, listen and give others a chance to influence you. If you want to influence others, you must also be willing to be influenced by them. What a concept! In doing so, you create synergy in relationships. And this is where the true magic of influencing comes in: synergy is the phenomenon wherein cooperation between two or more people produces a combined effect greater than the sum of their individual efforts. This is precisely the kind of group energy and creativity that can transform middling organizations into dazzling powerhouses!

Step 4: Follow through.

After successfully influencing others and winning their support, follow through with the promises you made. Use motivating skills to keep your supporters on course, particularly those who joined your cause a bit reluctantly and might still be expressing disagreement of some kind. Candidly acknowledge those disagreements; don't minimize or brush them aside. Find a way to maintain the morale of each of your supporters, keep them challenged, focused, and on target. Demonstrate successful outcomes to your followers and continue to express your appreciation for their support. Finally, remember to have some fun and regularly celebrate team victories. Recognize superb individual contributions at these events. It's a powerful way to create lasting memories and deep emotional bonds within a group.

Good versus Bad Influence

Some executives simply never use influencing skills. As such, they don't do much damage, but they don't accomplish much, either. Far less benign are those who confuse "influencing" with bullying or strong-arm tactics; they cause a great deal of damage to an organization and its people. "The Bully" is a personality type we've all encountered, starting in Kindergarten. They elbow their way through every situation and can be counted on to hoard resources at the expense of others.

"Joan" was a senior vice president at a large insurance company who qualified for the "bully" label. Overtly abusive to her subordinates, she exercised influence as if flexing a muscle. She advanced her own personal agenda by displaying a "take-no-prisoners" attitude and employing both covert and overt means to engender fear in her people. But because she was unable to build healthy, trusting relationships (in the sense we've been discussing), she could not accomplish any larger organizational objectives. Her subordinates were paralyzed in matrix meetings because they had no authority to make decisions (or even suggestions) without consulting her first. Individuals, who had the nerve to ask for a decision to be reached during a meeting, would find themselves chastised and removed from the team. People understandably dreaded meeting or working with Joan. While she achieved some success in the short term, her freight train inevitably ran off the track. Joan's role at the company was minimized; eventually, she was encouraged to seek employment elsewhere.

"The Politician" is another type of poor influencer. Take "Henry," for example. He always had an agenda and tried to "influence" others covertly to join his side. Since he was a smooth talker, he was somewhat popular, but a number of people were bothered by his willingness to entangle others in activities many viewed as borderline unethical. The "vibes" surrounding Henry made people uncomfortable. His co-workers were right to trust their suspicions and gut feelings. It's very unethical for people to use coercion or deception, whether discreetly or overtly, to get what they want. Such behavior completely undermines group trust and cooperation and is anathema to building a solid team or for influencing people in a positive way.

Finally, there's the "Benevolent Leader." Unlike the bully or politician, these individuals have a flair for diplomacy. They're natural ambassadors, and in that role, they use their excellent influencing skills to build bridges between people and bring positive changes to their organizations. Benevolent leaders excel in their careers through their savvy ability to influence and motivate others for the greater good. They strongly value the principles of honesty and mutually supportive relationships. They understand and like other people; conversely, people like being around them. They generate enthusiasm and excitement. Benevolent leaders are "optimistic realists." They know the limits of what's possible, and they never ask for what people can't deliver (al-

Using Influence to Cross Silo Boundaries

In a siloed organization, people tend to hunker down and operate with a bunker mentality. To pull such an organization out of this morass, leaders must use all the influencing skills at their disposal. Their number-one job is to encourage collaboration and the sharing of information across lines. Breaking down barriers is the first step in initiating change and developing a culture in which resources are shared rather than hoarded. Typically, the influencing skills of people who've spent years in a siloed company are atrophied from lack of use. They haven't experienced the stimulating joy of working in an environment filled with diverse people who think and do things differently. Quite the reverse: they've spent years working in a tight-knit group of like-minded peers. Expect these poor souls to experience some "post-silo stress-disorder" as they emerge, blinking, from their sheltered existence. Be patient with them as they adjust to what may initially seem quite threatening. Coaching them in the art of influencing skills is a challenge, but a rewarding one. Through consistent and persistent use of the steps suggested above, amazing results can occur, and potential stars will certainly emerge.

though they're not afraid to push people out of their comfort zones in the interest of helping them grow as individuals). They engender trust among people at all levels of the organization, and these people, in turn, willingly step up and take risks on their behalf. And, once a task is accomplished and successful, a benevolent leader is the first to give accolades to the supporters who made it possible.

Measuring Increased Effectiveness at Influencing

A soft, subjective way to measure influencing skills is by listening to feedback from subordinates. A good influencer is usually referred to as a pleasure to work with, someone people look forward to seeing on Monday morning (T.G.I.M.!). Coworkers enjoy sharing their passion for projects with them and trustingly follow their directions. People continually volunteer to join their teams and special projects. Although

Influencing, Negotiating, and Persuading

Managers sometimes mistake negotiating for influencing. They train their people in negotiation skills, but sadly neglect other aspects of their influence "curriculum." Negotiation is just one type of influence. The same is true for persuading, which we'll define here as "building a case on why something should happen." It's an important skill to possess, but certainly not the only one. Take, for example, listening and asking good questions. Those two abilities are absolutely essential in building good relationships and communicating the big-picture view of a specific goal or vision. Versatile and EI-savvy executives employ a wide variety of influence skills, based on their ability to read a given situation or audience. This is a class one never graduates from. The very best students continually learn new and more effective ways to influence others, and teach those skills to the people coming up behind them.

subjective, this is a great preliminary method to gauge an individual leader's influencing skills.

A more empirical way to measure effectiveness is by examining a leader's track record. A good influencer attracts the best and brightest talent, knows how to motivate them and obtains consistently stellar results. Projects are completed on time, within scope, on budget, and to the satisfaction of all concerned with significant ROI. "People find great value in influencing skills," says Vengel. "Companies' measurements have shown that 63 percent of people trained in influencing skills still used those skills some years later, while only 30 percent persistently used the skills learned in other types of classes."

Influencing the Next Generation

Passing along influencing skills to the next generation of leaders is as easy as being a good role model. When you use constructive, positive influence to garner resources and support, your direct reports will learn to do the same. Bullies eventually succumb to peer pressure by either changing their ways or leaving the organization. Leaders skilled in influencing, intentionally create opportunities for direct reports to flex their influencing muscles. Start by delegating as many meaningful activities as possible, and put your junior executives in charge of teams and projects that allow them to practice their influencing skills by accomplishing specific goals. Remember that failure is often the best teacher (that's why it's called "trial and error"). Use constructive and consistent feedback as you coach subordinates to consecutively higher achievement and confidence levels. It's a two-step process: model behavior and teach through application.

Additional Resources

Harnessing the Science of Persuasion by Robert B. Cialdini, Harvard Business Review, www.harvardbusiness.org, Product No. R0109D, 2001.

Influence: Science and Practice by Robert B. Cialdini, Allyn & Bacon, 2000

The Necessary Art of Persuasion by Jay Conger, Harvard Business Review, www.harvardbusiness.org, Product No. 4258, 2000.

What Makes a Leader? by Daniel Goleman, Harvard Business Review, www.harvardbusiness.org, Product No. R0401H, 2004.

Leadership That Gets Results by Daniel Goleman, Harvard Business Review, www.harvardbusiness.org, Product No. R00204, 2000.

Emotional Intelligence: Why It Can Matter More Than IQ by Daniel Goleman, Bantam, 1995.

Working with Emotional Intelligence by Daniel Goleman, Bantam, 2000.

The Influence Edge: How to Persuade Others to Help You Achieve Your Goals by Alan Vengel, Berrett-Koehler Publishers, 2001.

CHAPTER EIGHT
STRATEGIC THINKING
MAKES THE LEADER

Thinking is the hardest work there is. That is why so few people engage in it.
— Henry Ford

Most experts and scholars in business agree that one aspect of successful leadership comes from the ability to think—and act—strategically. But ask any one of them how to develop this extraordinarily important skill, and the answers vary considerably. It's not an easy subject to define, and when it comes to actually coaching leaders and managers in the area of strategic thinking, the topic's amorphous and elusive nature really begins to emerge. Imagine trying to explain to someone who doesn't swim how to swim. Imagine giving them a text on "the art" or "the science" of swimming. Chances are, although their conceptual understanding of swimming may advance, until they actually get into the water and try it, conceptual understanding alone will not be enough. The same holds true for strategic thinking. It must be first defined, then experienced. What exactly is strategic thinking? How best is it learned and taught? Defining it provides a good start to send your coachee down the right path towards understanding it, practicing it, and hopefully over time, mastering it.

To approach the topic, let's employ a little imagination. Picture yourself as a promising employee being groomed for a junior executive position in your organization. As you prepare for your move into a leadership position, one of the most difficult hurdles you'll face is a purely conceptual one. Let's refer to it here as a perceptual shifting of gears, a profound change from doing things right to doing the right thing—the classic shift from manager to leader. Doing things right is about managing processes. It requires technical/operational skills that advance tactical goals. On the other hand, doing the right thing refers to harnessing resources and leading people; it requires a long-term, broad, or big-picture approach.

In *The Leadership Pipeline: How to Build the Leadership Powered Company* (Jossey-Bass, 2000), authors Ram Charan, Stephen Drotter, and James Noel discuss the shifts in conceptual ability, activity, behavior, and thinking that employees make as they leave behind their positions as individual contributors in an organization and enter their new roles in management. Here's a typical ladder of management roles found in most organizations:

➢ Manager

➢ Manager of managers

➢ Functional manager

➢ Business manager

➢ Enterprise manager

Not making each of these leaps successfully is a common cause for derailment. Keep in mind that this leap is not just a behavioral jump or a change in how one allocates one's time; it's literally a conceptual leap.

What Is Strategic Thinking Anyway?

Strategic thinkers have an uncanny ability to perceive relationships. They see through complexities and understand the broad implications of issues. Their global perspective allows them to analyze opportunities and threats, and to better anticipate and plan for both the expected and unexpected. They visualize what might or could be, and are able to incorporate a far-sighted approach into their day-to-day, real-time responses to specific issues and challenges.

That's a tough order to fill for a new leader, and it's not something that is easily taught in college or in a three-day "strategic thinking" business seminar. Some new leaders need more help than others in this key area. For example, those who were promoted because they excelled as scientists, engineers, or technical experts need a great deal of coaching and practice to develop the art and science of strategic thinking.

For years, their jobs required them to be task-oriented and tactical, and because they got things done, they were ultimately promoted to leadership positions. But leadership isn't about technical skill sets. It's about getting things done through others.

Assessing Strategic Thinking Skills

Although 360 Degree surveys are a superb tool for assessing coachees in general, they don't work well in measuring an emerging leader's strategic thinking skills. Mary Boren, an executive coach and former senior HR director at a large biotech company, offers the following illustration from her own experience: "I was asked to coach Randall, a new executive who lacked strategic thinking skills (according to his boss, Teresa). I first interviewed Teresa and asked how she planned to measure Randall in that regard." Teresa responded that she would look for qualitative changes in his presentations and project plans as indicators of growth in his strategic-thinking abilities. Boren recalls that she immediately felt Teresa was on the wrong track.

"From my own perspective," says Boren, "preparing a successful plan does not represent the ability to think strategically." All Teresa actually planned to measure was Randall's ability to develop a plan that conformed to Teresa's own time-line expectations. In other words, Teresa was mistaking the ability to present information about projects using a certain format, scope, and time horizon with true strategic thinking. Those are tactical skills, however, not strategic abilities. It is doubtful Randall would get the coaching he needed when the tools used to measure his progress were measuring the wrong abilities.

"When a coach is asked to help people to learn to think strategically, it can be a slippery request," says Boren. "You first have to elicit the criteria the boss or other stakeholder is using to evaluate the coachee's strategic thinking skills. A 360 Degree survey would not work because everyone's perception of the coachee's strategic thinking skills will be different, depending on people's own perceptions, expectations, time horizons, and definitions of strategic thinking."

When Boren is asked to coach an individual in strategic thinking, her first step, surprisingly enough, is not to meet with her coachee. Rather, Boren seeks out the person in the company who raised the subject of the coachee's inability to think strategically. Boren then interviews that person and asks questions like these: "Who in this company is considered to be an excellent strategic thinker? What are the components of that person's strategic thinking skill that impress you; in other words, what is it you see or hear that leads you to believe that this individual is a great strategic thinker?"

These are important questions to ask because the answers are different for every leader and every organization. Everyone evaluates strategic thinking skills according to their own criteria. Further complicating the issue is the fact that as organizations mature, they tend to shift from being fairly near-term focused—at least in some respects—to thinking in an integrated way as they become more aware of their enterprise-wide accountabilities.

When it comes to interviewing coachees, asking nonspecific questions is the best way to determine skill levels. For example, if you want to find out in what time horizon they operate, ask: "What do you think the long-range trends are in the marketplace?" or "Tell me what your thoughts are when you think about long-range planning?" The term "long-range" is purposely unspecific. For some individuals, long-range means three months, for others it may be three years or twenty years. Ask the question and let people fill in the blanks with their own definitions, in contexts that make sense to them. Do not ask directly, "How do you define short-term or long-term?" because you will only get a textbook answer. The idea is to gain insights about their strategic thinking processes by a decidedly indirect route. Try to avoid questions that telegraph what you want to hear. Go in with an open mind and non-leading questions, and let the coachees define how their minds operate.

Also, putting individuals or groups through either SWOT analysis (Strengths, Weaknesses, Opportunities, Threats) or SPOT analysis (Strengths, Problems, Opportunities, Threats) is a good way to assess strategic thinking skills. This can be done with questionnaires that ask questions like these:

> Over the next three years, what top three trends do you see in _____? (Fill in environmental scan areas, such as demographics, the economy, the marketplace, politics, the industry, the competition, etc.).

> What are the top three internal strengths in this organization?

> What are its top three internal weaknesses (or problems)?

> What are the organization's top three external opportunities?

> What are the top three external threats facing the organization?

> What single change would have the most positive impact on this organization's effectiveness?

Again, the language of the questions should be kept unspecific to allow a person's thinking to follow its natural course. Compile the survey data and get everyone to discuss it. It's always surprising how differently people view things and what sort of time horizons they frame their thinking in. For example, when people are asked to describe the trends they predict in politics, some people will consider only the United States, others will think globally, and still others will focus on the politics within their department. All perspectives are valid because they each have impact, although in different ways. Learning to respect individual differences is essential in this regard. As one gains a better understanding of the wide variety in these conceptual horizons and perspectives, the topic of strategic thinking becomes much less slippery and elusive.

"My belief is that everyone thinks strategically," says Boren. "For example, we think about how we're going to pay our taxes next year, or we think about the implications of moving to another city. But people have different time horizons and different habits in that regard. It's just a matter of coaching them to map their abilities across other areas in which they may be thinking less strategically—at least according to someone else's opinion."

Elements of Strategic Thinking

Despite individual differences in perspective and time horizon, there are a few components of strategic thinking on which most experts agree. They include:

> ➤ The ability to mentally project one's department, company, goal, or plan along a time horizon of adequate length and relevance, as judged by the unique standards of a given organization. This ability is a prerequisite for strategic planning.

> ➤ A willingness to steer away from relatively easier, tactical, short-term "comfort zone" activities. Let's face it: long-term, strategic thinking challenges one's intellect and creativity and can be downright exhausting! It's tempting (and all too easy) for managers to spend their time putting out company fires rather than engaging in strategic, long-term thinking.

> ➤ The capacity to keep the scope of an initiative broad rather than specific, tactical, or narrow.

> ➤ A talent for considering many functional areas in problem solving and decision making, rather than just one business unit or one section of the operation.

> ➤ Skill in seeing the relationships between people and process, and between specific individuals, teams, and other parts of the value chain (suppliers, distributors, and customers).

> ➤ A mind-set focused beyond one's immediate goals and the means to achieve them. This farsightedness considers such short-term goals only as they relate to the mission or vision.

> ➤ A facility for balancing long-term strategic issues and goals with short-term priorities.

➢ The discipline to define one's destination before launching an activity or setting out on a path, combined with the ability to clearly articulate why it's the right destination.

➢ Proficiency in creating a vision and mission, and achieving them within acceptable time frames, with minimal risk and optimal use of resources (human and otherwise).

➢ Accountability combined with a systemic approach to important issues. For example, making sure that the activities of the people in one part of the organization do not hinder productivity in another section.

➢ Sensitivity to early warning signals of changes in the environment, including demographics, politics, regulations, and the global marketplace.

➢ Consistent engagement with other leaders in the organization, especially as it relates to decisions regarding the course and implementation of an unfolding strategic plan.

On the flip side, you probably are not good at strategic thinking if the following describes your management style:

➢ **Micromanaging.** Everybody falls into this trap from time to time. But chronic micromanagement demonstrates a failure to set strategy for others and prevents them from learning how to work on their own.

➢ **Following rather than leading.** Ah, yes, a comfortable workplace where nobody has to think...How relaxing! People just do their jobs day after day, following orders without an end in mind. Clear strategy is lacking. So, too, are profitability, productivity and, well, any signs of life. Scotty, beam us outta here!

➢ **Crisis management with no end in sight.** These leaders are always putting out fires and flying by the seat of their pants. The prevailing attitude is, "We'll take it as it comes and figure it out as we always have." (Sounds like a description of the problem rather than the solution!) One person's lack of planning is always becoming another's emergency. Managers and leaders who work this way create horrible stress and burnout in the organization. For adrenaline and drama junkies only!

> **Weekend warrior strategic planning.** You know the drill: at the annual offsite retreat, all the executives in the organization get "strategic religion," but forget to bring it with them to the office on Monday. "Don't worry," they say. "Someone's writing it up in a strategic planning document," which nobody ever reads, of course.

> **Lone Rangerism.** These isolated leaders suffer from a striking absence of buy-in from subordinates and peers. This is often due to a vision that lacks vibrancy or planning that fails to integrate all levels of the organization. Or maybe people just don't like these leaders very much (or all three).

All joking aside, these are real problems that plague real organizations—far too many of them. These misguided leaders make life miserable for everyone who works for them, and they profoundly undermine their organization's productivity and bottom line. If this describes your organization, don't despair! Help is on the way.

Coaching for Strategic Thinking

Mark McCormack, author of *What They Don't Teach You at Harvard Business School: Notes From a Street-Smart Executive* (Bantam Reissue Edition, 1986), states, "A Master's in business can sometimes block an ability to master experience. Many of the M.B.A.'s we hired were either congenitally naïve or victims of their business training. The result was a kind of real-life learning disability—a failure to read people properly or to size up situations and an uncanny knack for forming the wrong perceptions."

If this description applies to emerging leaders in your organization, they may need to overcome the limiting mindset created by academic training. It will probably require self-study prior to, or concurrent with, actual coaching in strategic thinking. An excellent set of tools can be found in Michael J. Gelb's book *How to Think Like Leonardo da Vinci* (Dell, 2000). The book outlines thinking exercises that illustrate "the Seven Da Vincian Principles" (from *How to Think Like Leonardo da Vinci*, p. 9):

1. **Curiosita**—An insatiably curious approach to life and an unrelenting quest for continuous learning.

2. **Dimostrazione**—A commitment to test knowledge through experience, persistence, and a willingness to learn from mistakes.

3. **Sensazione**—The continual refinement of the senses, especially sight, as the means to enliven experience.

4. **Sfumato** (literally "Going up in Smoke")—A willingness to embrace ambiguity, paradox, and uncertainty.

5. **Arte/Scienza**—The development of the balance between science and art, logic and imagination. "Whole-brain" thinking.

6. **Corporalita**—The cultivation of grace, ambidexterity, fitness, and poise.

7. **Connessione**—A recognition of and appreciation for the interconnectedness of all things and phenomena (also known as "systems thinking").

The last of these, systems thinking, ties into the big-picture view that is so critical for leaders. Few of us are born with that ability. Emerging leaders must be properly coached in order to change their perspective from process to systems-oriented thinking. Have your coachees practice the following skills:

➤ Identify all the stakeholders potentially involved in a situation.

➤ Probe beneath the surface and gather information from different stakeholders.

➤ Ask open-ended questions.

➤ Define problems from the perspective of each stakeholder.

➤ Identify the work processes involved when solving specific problems and in making the most of opportunities that arise.

➤ Recognize the broad implications of issues.

➤ Determine the important strategic issues for specific areas of the organization.

➤ Break key issues down into hierarchically ordered priorities.

➤ Examine potential decisions in light of how they may affect or be affected by key strategic issues.

➤ Elicit far-reaching ideas from peers and subordinates.

➤ View competitive threats and opportunities through a strategic lens.

➤ Focus on a future-oriented, big-picture framework rather than minutiae when interacting with senior leadership.

➤ Unleash creativity as a guiding force in the company.

➤ Develop contingency and mitigation plans that anticipate trends in an ever-changing future.

Effective, strategic-thinking leaders often attribute their success to knowing the right questions to ask as opposed to having all the answers. Help your coachees hone their questioning minds by encouraging them to frame their discussions with strategic queries like these:

➤ What is our long-term goal for this division?

➤ Where are we today in relation to this goal?

➤ How can we get from where we are to where we want to be?

➤ What resources are at our disposal to help in this effort?

> What obstacles may hinder us?

> How might our environment (internal or external) change in such a way as to necessitate a modification in our approach or long-term goal?

> How can we measure success along the way?

> How will we know when we have achieved our goal?

> Once we have achieved this goal, what might be the next goal looking even further ahead, and the next goal after that for the very distant future?

Ensure that your coachees have sufficient exposure to senior leadership to practice and demonstrate their growing ability to see to the horizon. Have them schedule review dates to meet with senior executives in order to discuss current and relevant issues. Prior to these meetings, help the coachees clarify their big-picture views

Special Tip

Create a culture that encourages strategic thinking. Establishing employee bonus plans for those who meet annual goals tends to work against the attempt to create a long-term, more strategic orientation.

of the issues. Set aside practice times in which they can use you as a sounding board to rehearse the messages they want conveyed.

When meeting with coachees or emerging leaders, always ask "high-yield" questions that prompt them to think deeply and strategically. Jack Welch and other senior executives at GE used their "Session C" process (a formal multilevel review of organizational performance and leadership assessment) in that way. Here's a good example of a high-yield question to ask presenters regarding one of their conclusions: "What other data might exist to support your argument?" To be effective, high-yield queries should be non-threatening and transparent. The purpose here is to clarify an issue for everyone's benefit, not to engage in "gotcha" investigative journalism! The most effective high-yield questions get everyone in the room to think, not just the presenter.

Strategic Thinking and Planning

The ability to think strategically must be paired with strategic planning in order to create followers who will help achieve the vision. Although an individual can think strategically by himself or herself, strategic planning is the process of bringing strategic thinkers together to brainstorm ideas for the future, reach decisions on which ideas to implement, and develop creative, proactive plans to turn them into reality.

Strategic planning, as one would expect, also requires effective follow-up. Even the most brilliant strategic thinking and planning will result in little more than an interesting academic exercise unless followed by careful execution. And, obviously, executives aren't paid to produce abstractions, no matter how fascinating they may be. It's important for strategic thinkers and planners to always remember that they are laying the groundwork for work that will be undertaken by real people in the real world. One of the primary reasons why strategic plans fail in execution is that leaders didn't properly visualize what it would take to turn their vision into a worthy and value-producing organizational endeavor.

Case Study: Getting to the Big Picture

Jerry was a manager in the energy industry one level below the executive ranks. His 360 Degree assessment revealed high competency in managing details, coupled with a strong (and not surprising) tendency to think tactically rather than strategically. His strategic-thinking coaching plan focused initially on increasing Jerry's ability to see issues from the 30,000-foot view. He then was encouraged to widen the scope of his other conceptual abilities, comprehend the interrelationships of circumstances, and to stay focused on critical areas. It also meant learning some self-discipline and avoiding falling back into his old comfort zones (focusing on the details—and getting lost in them).

Jerry's development was helped a great deal by increasing his exposure to leadership in a more consistent fashion. Good coaching in all of these areas helped him shift his thinking from a tactical orientation to a strategic one.

Jerry's 360 Degree evaluation had also indicated work was needed in his stress management skills and his ability to adapt to changing conditions. Jerry's coach taught him how to delegate tasks to his staff. She also taught him how to coach them rather than trying to do it all himself. In the process, he decreased his workload by 25 percent, which created more time for strategic thinking. By increasing his strategic thinking skills he was able to anticipate roadblocks and delegate tasks in response to them rather than reacting to them. As a result, his stress levels decreased markedly.

After differentiating himself from the management ranks through the development of new strategic-level skills, Jerry was promoted to an almost exclusively strategic executive role in the company as an IT liaison. Although he previously had a strong background in both IT and the division's specialty, his promotion to this highly respected role resulted from the development of his new strategic skills. His initial assessment played an important role in this story, by first identifying his strengths and weaknesses. With that important roadmap in hand, Jerry and his boss/coach could then move towards the development of greater, more meaningful, and valuable strategic skills.

Additional Resources:

What They Don't Teach You at Harvard Business School: Notes from a Street-Smart Executive by Mark H. McCormack, Bantam Reissue Edition, 1986.

How to Think Like Leonardo da Vinci: Seven Steps to Genius Every Day by Michael J. Gelb, Dell, 2000.

The Art of War: The Oldest Military Treatise in the World by Sun-Tzu, Running Press Book Publishers, 2003.

The GE Way Fieldbook: Jack Welch's Battle Plan for Corporate Revolution by Robert Slater, McGraw-Hill, 1999.

Built to Last: Successful Habits of Visionary Companies by Jim Collins and Jerry I. Porras, Perseus Books, 1997.

The Leadership Pipeline: How to Build the Leadership Powered Company by Ram Charan, Stephen Drotter, and James Noel, Jossey-Bass, 2000.

CHAPTER NINE

REAL DIVERSITY FOR THE NEW MILLENNIUM

If we continue to do what we've always done, we'll continue to get what we've always got.
— Albert Einstein

Here's a quick word association game: What comes to your mind when you hear the term "workplace diversity"? If your response is "race, gender, or ethnicity," give yourself five points for a correct answer. Then deduct three points for being a bit narrow-minded.

Don't worry. We won't share your score with anyone else, and please, don't beat yourself up. This isn't some new and sneaky "political correctness" litmus test! The point of the exercise is simply to illustrate how the subject—human diversity in the business world—has expanded in scope in the past decade (at least we hope it has). Yes, diversity is certainly concerned with the topics of race, gender, and ethnicity, but it shouldn't stop there. It encompasses many other vital areas related to individual differences, points of view, and competence.

The Meaning of Diversity

The long-established definitions of workplace diversity, which focus on race, gender, and ethnicity, make it easy to categorize people according to obvious characteristics. That, in turn, makes the measuring and reporting of an organization's demographics convenient and simple. Companies that rank high in these categories love to show off their demographic statistics. It makes for good press, particularly when a company wins a slot on one of the many "Lists of Top Companies. . ." published by Forbes, DiversityInc, and others.

Narrowly focused, traditional demographic diversity initiatives, however, often represent little more than a superficial effort at regulatory compliance or public relations. In all fairness, such mechanisms—

even the most cynical—have the capacity to measurably increase social justice and equality, and that's a good thing. But research over the last few years has demonstrated this notable trend: a diversity culture limited to race, gender, and ethnicity has few, if any measurable business benefits. Think about that for a moment and consider it in light of the organizational "diversity paradigms" with which you're probably familiar.

Here's a recap of what that groundbreaking research indicated: Workplace teams with a balanced mixture of race, gender, and ethnicity tend to achieve outcomes virtually undistinguishable from those of teams that were not so equitably balanced. This leads many experts to conclude that American businesspeople, regardless of color, ethnicity, and gender, are extraordinarily similar in the way they think, work together, and solve problems. This is particularly true when the individuals are of approximately the same age, socioeconomic background, and education. What's behind this phenomenon? The answer is culture, and not of the corporate ilk. Rather, it's because the subjects studied were all steeped in our national culture. In some fashion, it appears, the fabled American melting pot seems to be doing its job pretty well.

Defining Diversity

Race, gender and ethnicity are only three components of a much broader type of diversity—the diversity of individual differences and points of view. Obviously, that includes other factors, including age, national origin, religion, sexual orientation, and disability. But beyond that, it extends to personalities, marital status, beliefs, cultural norms, and the full scope of individual qualities and characteristics that make each human being unique.

While this definition may make diversity more elusive and complicated, the business benefits are clear. Team members who exhibit different personalities, styles, ways of thinking, and approaches to problem solving are more likely to challenge each other's assumptions and arrive at better solutions. It's the ideal breeding ground for the true innovation and creativity demanded by today's marketplace—an environment as diverse as it is global. Our current marketplace requires diverse solutions, solutions which are simply beyond the capacity of a company in which everyone thinks alike, has the same education and background, and views everything through a similar cultural framework. When everyone is in the same box, thinking outside of it is virtually impossible.

Creating a Diverse Workforce

Achieving optimal diversity—like all change initiatives—is a matter of taking a series of logical steps: assess the current state, define the goal, conduct a gap analysis, close the gap, and measure results. Let's examine how that might play out in a typical organization:

Step 1: Measure the current state.

Statistics work well when the goal is to measure traditional characteristics such as race, gender, age, and ethnicity. But other tools are necessary to gauge and assess more elusive characteristics, such as:

➢ Potential challenges and barriers to increased diversity (from mild stereotyping to outright discrimination).

➢ Prevailing employee attitudes and beliefs. A good example of this is the mistaken notion held by many people that diversity equals affirmative action.

➢ Indicators of underlying resentments. (Example: unspoken anger towards recently promoted minority staff members.)

➢ Expressed or unspoken assumptions concerning different groups ("GenXers," "bean counters," "good old boys," "geeks," etc.).

For the most comprehensive results, use surveys and assessment tools like the Myers-Briggs Type Indicator or DiSC. They can appraise and evaluate differences in personality and style and other less tangible characteristics. (Refer to the Appendix for information on these and other assessments.)

Step 2: Define goals.

It's important to clarify, at the outset, exactly what benefits your organization hopes to achieve by increasing diversity. In most cases, companies are interested in the positive impact that greater diversity would have on employees, stockholders, the marketplace, and the community at large. Quantify how diversity would need to be increased in order to achieve those benefits. Decide which organizational qualities or types of people the company should cultivate and attract. This may involve, for example, actively recruiting younger people, women, and individuals with work experience outside the United States, or those possessing valuable insights relating to customer demographics and cultural differences. What areas of the company are in need of diversity or sensitivity training? These are some of the critical issues organizations will want to consider when initiating a strategic approach to diversity.

Step 3: Create a plan to close the gap.

Specific plans will vary from one organization to another, depending on current diversity environments and future goals, but here are a few general guidelines that apply to nearly every situation:

➤ Form a diversity taskforce to spearhead the effort. This is especially important if a far-reaching diversity initiative is necessary. The taskforce should be as truly diverse as possible in itself, accurately representing a vertical and horizontal cross-section of the actual organization, its current state, and its anticipated future needs. In addition, it will probably be wise to include external advisors who can contribute perspectives not represented internally.

➤ Develop a hiring mechanism that will increase diversity. Use assessments to identify candidates with the desired personalities and qualities. When interviewing candidates, your greatest challenge will be to overcome the natural tendency to hire like-minded individuals. Easy to say, but hard to do! We all enjoy talking to and interacting with people who are like us. Not only that, we get along better with them; interpersonal conflicts arise far less often among people who share common demographic qualities. With that in mind, here's a suggestion: approach recruitment with the expressed intention of creating a truly diverse team, including people with diverging points of view and dissimilar backgrounds. This might include people who lack the "industry experience" so often required in employment ads, or people who work and conduct business in ways that may seem odd, exotic, or downright strange yet practical and results-oriented. Next time you need to hire from the outside, take a closer look at the job posting. Is it so narrow that it will attract only "good fits" (i.e., clones of everyone else in the organization)?

➢ Carefully consider an individual's temperament, especially when promoting to executive positions internally. Look beyond the usual candidates and not just with regard to obvious demographics. Avoid the temptation to choose the traditionally obvious "rising star." You know the type: young barnstormers who jump in the spotlight at every available opportunity, making sure everyone can see what a great job they're doing. There is another brand of talent that is often overlooked— individuals who eschew fanfare and the limelight. These low-key individuals often possess a strong work ethic, know how to marshal resources, get the job done on time and on budget, and give credit where credit is due. Yes, they may approach things a bit differently from the barnstormers—and thank goodness for that! How many show-offs can one company stand? The truth is: these humble performers tend to represent the real backbone of an organization, generally producing, in their unassuming ways, results that rival their barnstorming counterparts. Not only that, they bring a refreshingly different viewpoint and chemistry to their respective teams. Now, that's diversity that pays dividends.

Where are these unsung heroes and valuable future leaders found? Look for them in support positions behind VPs, team leaders, and project leaders. They're the ones who quietly work to make their superiors successful day in and day out. They generally possess excellent working relationships and networks within the organization. More than likely, they've also earned the trust and credibility of everyone around them. But by their nature, they tend not to toot their own horns, so it's easy to overlook them. Granted, not every unsung hero has leadership potential, but some have simply never been given the opportunity to stretch. Conduct an objective assessment of their abilities and true intentions. Those who exhibit potential should then be given ample opportunity to prove themselves as part of a diverse group or project team.

➤ Provide diversity training to raise awareness and to develop skills employees can use in an environment of increased diversity. Here again, do not limit that training simply to the current model of "expected diversity sensitivity"— broaden it as defined here and stretch!

➤ Utilize cross-training and rotational assignments as part of leadership preparation. Expose up-and-coming executives to as many departments and individuals as possible. Have them run business units that are totally foreign to them. Show them how to mentor other individuals whose approaches are different from their own. The more experience they gain by interacting with diverse individuals and work styles, the better. It will force them to stretch and grow as individuals and professionals while giving you the opportunity to assess them in a wide variety of situations.

➤ Assign mentors from within and across lines of race, gender, and ethnicity. Mentoring is an excellent complement to cross-training when developing future leaders. Without a doubt, a member of a minority can be a good role model for an emerging leader of the same background, but limiting mentor/mentee relationships to such homogenous pairings will stop true diversity in its tracks.

For other strategies for building a diverse workforce, refer to the Society for Human Resource Management's Diversity Toolkit, www. shrm.org.

Step 4: Measure results.

The benefits of increased diversity are far-reaching and multifaceted. The greater the change in the company, the more significant the benefits are for employees, customers, stockholders, and the community. The marketplace, for instance, will gain more innovative products created by a company's diverse product development team. Customer satisfaction and retention may increase as a result of varied sales and service divisions. These benefits in turn will increase ROI and revenues leading to greater shareholder value. Communities tend to have a higher regard for companies possessing greater internal variety—not from a position of political correctness, but rather, because the company represents a truer cross-section of the community itself. Such organizations also provide a greater number and range of employment opportunities in their immediate region. Finally, local nonprofits and community organizations benefit from a heterogeneous pool of executives available for board service.

The benefits of a diverse organization are wide-ranging and substantial. They include fewer EEO complaints, lower turnover, and absenteeism rates, greater job satisfaction, less conflict, higher team spirit, and increased loyalty to the company.

Quantifying the results and ROI of increased diversity is more challenging than measuring less complex (but more tangible) business endeavors. However, practical tools do exist. Microsoft, for example, has developed a customized index to measure specific diversity initiatives over time. It quantifies the relative success or failure of the initiative and its overall impact on the organization, and can track the performance of complex affirmative action programs (and outreach efforts) as a way of analyzing and communicating EEO and AAP information. Don't take shortcuts though. Measuring tools that provide simplistic data or cookie-cutter results can be misleading and will ultimately detract from (or substantially damage) an organization's diversity initiative.

Exercises

1. **Create diversity "yardsticks."** Gather a diverse team of emerging leaders. In selecting members, remember to use the new, broader definition of diversity, not just race, gender, and ethnicity. Ask the team to develop a number of measurements that can assess the potential business benefits of increased diversity (in its new definition) within the company.

2. **Establish appropriate hiring benchmarks.** Assemble a diverse team of emerging leaders for the purpose of discussing the following case:

> During an offsite meeting to establish standards for individuals being considered for leadership development, an Asian American executive raised an interesting issue. While working with several Asian American managers who had not been in the United States very long, he noticed that most exhibited marked cultural differences. For example, they lacked certain traits often critical for leadership success, such as being assertive and outspoken. In some Asian cultures, the executive noted, these traits are considered impolite and unacceptable.

> How would your team resolve this problem? Should the bar be lowered to meet the cultural needs of these Asian American colleagues? By doing so, would it encourage substandard performance? Or, should those culturally disadvantaged managers be mentored and empowered to overcome traits that obstruct their advancement? In other words, should they be trained to be more like everyone else (i.e., "corporate, cultural assimilation")?

From Diversity to Consensus

In some companies, the traditional approach to diversity trips up new leaders, especially those who lack experience and expertise managing a workforce composed of races, ethnicities, and styles differing from their own. Managers and leaders in large energy utility companies routinely face such difficulties because their organizations are among the most diverse. FORTUNE magazine's list of the fifty most diverse companies includes Sempra Energy, Southern California Edison, PNM Resources, PG&E, Consolidated Edison, DTE Energy, and Pepco. The Fortune list committee takes into consideration items such as the following:

> The number of minorities in the workforce

> How many minority members sit on the board of directors

> Hiring and firing rates for minorities

> How managers are held accountable for minority hiring, promotion, and retention

As of 2006, one of these utility companies boasted a 60 percent "minority" employee ratio, with an employee demographic that included African Americans, Asian Americans, Latinos, and some Native Americans. The remaining 40 percent of the workforce was comprised of Caucasian men and women. Many of the company's less experienced leaders struggled with this relatively high rate of diversity, but they found themselves handicapped when it came to bridging what were, to them, significant cultural and ethnic barriers. The company responded by implementing a mentoring program in which less experienced leaders could seek the guidance of seasoned colleagues. Frankly, even though in theory the program should have had a high success rate, the results were mixed. The continued imposition of both HR standards and board member "requests" for even more diversity (an oxymoron at this stage with 60 percent of the workforce representing "minorities" who are now the majority!), along with the lack of freedom for mentees and others to hire and develop executives based on organizational need, rather than imposed quotas, put a stranglehold on the program.

Regardless of industry, managing a diverse workforce can lead to occasional and, at times, significant friction and conflict. Maintaining harmony in such potentially divisive environments takes every leadership skill discussed in this book—communication and motivational skills, influencing, prowess as a coach and mentor, and in particular, dexterity in conflict management.

A word of warning: some groups and teams can become so diverse that they cannot reach consensus (hence, they cannot effectively function). Sometimes this problem is caused by managers who so revel in the terrific energy often found in a diverse group that they forget there is work to do. Encourage these managers to keep constructive conflict to a moderate level, especially if it has been leading to frequent consensus-related logjams.

The *Harvard Business Review* article "How Management Teams Can Have a Good Fight," authored by Kathleen M. Eisenhardt, Jean L. Kahwajy, and L.J. Bourgeois, suggests five steps to encourage healthy debate among diverse teams while keeping disagreement constructive:

1. Assemble a heterogeneous team. Include diverse ages, genders, functional backgrounds, and industry experience. If everyone in the executive meeting looks alike and sounds alike, then chances are excellent they'll probably think alike, too.

2. Meet together as a team regularly and often. Team members who know one another well and know where everybody stands on specific issues, are in the best position to argue effectively. Frequent interaction builds a mutual confidence and familiarity that helps team members express their dissent in appropriateways.

3. Encourage team members to assume roles beyond their obvious product, geographic, or functional responsibilities. When devil's advocates, sky-gazing visionaries, and action-oriented executives work together effectively, it increases the chance that all sides of an issue will be thoroughly examined and considered.

4. Apply multiple mindsets to every issue. Try role-playing, putting yourself in the competition's shoes and conducting

war games. Such techniques create fresh perspectives, engage team members, and spur interest in problem solving.

5. Actively manage conflict. Don't let the team acquiesce too soon or too easily. Identify and dispel apathy early. Don't confuse a lack of conflict with agreement. Often, what passes for consensus is really disengagement.

Intervene quickly and assertively when a team shows signs of falling apart or getting mired in "diversity paralysis." Help team members understand the differences and similarities in their points of view and coach them to consensus. Good mediation skills are a real plus in these situations.

True Diversity for a Global Marketplace

It comes as no surprise that globalization is creating a more diverse marketplace in which companies must operate. However, many organizations have been caught flat-footed by the growing diversity that globalization is creating within their own workplaces. The fact is: up-and-coming leaders who don't know how to manage true diversity—in both the traditional and the broader sense—will be at a profound disadvantage. If they don't become adept at working across the lines of gender, race, ethnicity, culture, age, style, and individuality, they'll not be successful in meeting the demands of today's global markets.

It takes true organizational courage to revisit the traditional model of diversity and blend it with a broader, more unconventional, but meaningful and pragmatic view. The goal here is for each company to develop a hybrid approach that works for the organization, its customers, shareholders, and surrounding community. Companies short-change themselves when they undertake diversity initiatives merely to satisfy regulatory requirements or qualify for a "Top Fifty Whatever" list. Take the high road! Strive to achieve true diversity of thinking. Elicit, engage, and demand the very best from all your people. Be passionate and take risks. In doing the right thing, you'll develop an organization that attracts the very best employees, where people love their jobs. You'll also be laying the groundwork for creating the best possible products and services for your customers.

Additional Resources

Society for Human Resource Management: Diversity Toolkit, www.shrm.org

Measuring the Results of a Diversity Initiative, www.shrm.org

What Are the Components of a Successful Diversity Initiative? www.shrm.org

Ten Strategies for Achieving a More Diverse Membership, www.shrm.org

"How Management Teams Can Have a Good Fight" by Kathleen M. Eisenhardt, Jean L. Kahwajy, and L.J. Bourgeois, *Harvard Business Review*, 1997 www.harvardbusiness.org,.

Responses to Diversity: Approaches and Initiatives by Anne M. McMahon, Ph.D., SHRM White Paper, www.shrm.org, May 2006.

Managing Diversity: Toward a Globally Inclusive Workplace by Dr. Michalle E. Mor Barak, Sage Publications, 2005.

Overcoming Resistance to a Successful Diversity Effort by Tina Rasmussen, ASTD Case Study, www.astd.org, Product Code 71040012.

"Diversity Finds Its Place" by Robert Rodriguez, *HR Magazine*, www.shrm.org, Vol. 51, No. 8, August 2006.

CHAPTER TEN

CHANGE MANAGEMENT:
Developing a Flexible, High-Trust Culture

Charisma becomes the undoing of leaders. It makes them inflexible,
convinced of their own infallibility, unable to change.

— Peter Drucker

The late Peter Drucker called "leading change" the key management challenge of the twenty-first century. Not surprisingly, there is no shortage of books and articles giving advice on how to manage change "the right way." Yet, despite all of the lessons and well-intentioned advice, organizations still have not mastered change management. Perhaps the reason is not due to lack of good processes, but rather to unresolved challenges involving "softer" issues, namely the ever-elusive human equation. A great deal of evidence—both anecdotal and scholarly—finally supports that observation.

In the Introduction to this book, we noted a new vulnerability among today's leaders. They are running as fast as they can, and yet, it never seems fast enough. One of the reasons for this never-ending treadmill is the constant, rapid change in both internal and external conditions. It's a vicious cycle. The more quickly the environment changes, the more organizations struggle to accommodate the new circumstances.

Therefore what's needed is not another new change management process, but rather a better understanding of how to develop an environment conducive to change, along with the abilities needed to both lead and deal with change—specifically, flexibility and adaptability.

Got CQ (Change Quotient)?

When it comes to leading and managing change, it's a waste of time to focus on undoing past mistakes. Instead, it's better for today's leaders to focus their efforts on coaching and mentoring the next generation of leaders so that they can sidestep those historic traps. This isn't to say that the "old guard" can't improve its own performance. Far from it! By its very nature, coaching is a two-way street, with both coach and coachee learning from one another. It creates a perfect learning environment for both to improve their own change management performance, while developing the same skills in their coachees.

Like so many leadership abilities, the skills needed to lead change have little to do with technical proficiency. Instead, leading change requires what I refer to as a high "CQ" (Collaborative Quotient). CQ focuses on the often slippery slope of human emotions and reactions. That's because organizations are not edifices or collections of processes; they are groups of people interacting with one another inside and outside the company. And since leadership is about accomplishing things through others, change is primarily about motivating and enabling people to do things differently.

If this simple fact is overlooked, change initiatives flounder. Here's a typical scenario. A large (and very expensive) management consulting firm is hired to spearhead an expansive multimillion-dollar change initiative revolving around the implementation of the latest "revolutionary" new system or process. Much training ensues and a buzz of excitement fills the air, accompanied by some seemingly impressive initial outcomes. Unfortunately, the early results are not real or sustainable, and after a year or two, the change initiatives are abandoned. What happened? Reality set in. Leaders who did not understand the people side of change focused the change initiative on the organization.

Why do leaders tend to be utterly infatuated with the latest change-du-jour? It's a mystery. Repeatedly, they introduce one "great" idea after another, often fueled by their favorite business guru's latest bestseller. All of this takes place in the face of tremendous resistance to change. The manifestations range from low morale to low productivity, symptoms that can be reduced to a common denominator: lack of trust. Root causes are varied and may include something as common as people being expected to adapt to new processes overnight after a merger or acquisition. But much more often, lack of trust derives from a constant barrage of change initiatives. After a while, people become fed up and shell-shocked by the constant parade of novelties and organizational metamorphoses. It's no wonder they respond with passive, if not active resistance. They are simply ill-informed about the proposed change, burned out by constant change (we all need some stability!), and, they are "over-processed."

The change-du-jour mentality dictates change, even when there is no clear or compelling reason for it. It amounts to constantly trying to fix something that "ain't broke." Far too often, leaders introduce a new process just because a competitor, the parent company, or an affiliate has done it. Neither a needs assessment nor cultural assessment precedes the demand for change. When headstrong leaders expect change, most employees and managers do not oppose them directly. Instead, they find safe and indirect ways to thwart compliance.

A related mistake often results from bringing in an outside resource that specializes in a specific change management process. If this process does not fit the company, or worse, the consultant lacks the requisite industry experience and credentials, resentment ensues and is never a good driver of change.

Poor communication is another reason why change initiatives fail, even when they are appropriate. Purpose, process, results, and expected benefits are never clearly articulated, and the outcome is almost always disastrous. Pulling the plug on a change initiative that is almost complete—for budgetary reasons or simply because someone at the top had a change of heart—is another way to devastate a workforce. It's a tremendous shock when the enormous human and emotional capital expended in an initiative is repudiated in such a manner. "Once burned, twice shy" the old saying goes and for good reason. These people are not likely to show enthusiasm when the next round of changes is proposed. A related common mistake is to complete a change process and then immediately begin another. If a specific change is not given time to settle in, people can't or don't realize its benefits. Understandably, they will be quite leery of future requests for change initiatives or programs.

In all of these types of situations, two primary perceptions emerge from employees and managers concerning the ill-fated change initiatives. They are:

➤ **The Ivory Tower Syndrome**—They came down from the ivory tower to tell us what to do, without asking for our input, ideas, and suggestions.

➤ **The Evil Dentist Experience**—The change process is like "having a root canal without anesthesia," very painful and to be avoided at all costs.

Yikes! Who would want to work in these types of organizations? The common thread here is a lack of sensitivity on the part of leaders—as to the needs of those most affected by the change—a mindset that breeds resistance among those who are asked to actually implement change or comply with "the new rules." When it comes to change initiatives, otherwise proficient leaders somehow lose their sensibilities and get so swept up in their big plans that they callously ignore the feelings of the people most affected by the change.

Flexibility Comes in Many Forms

The planning and execution of change requires flexibility on the part of both leaders and followers. While there are many different types of flexibility, one very important one is flexibility of style in presenting a compelling case for a change initiative and its benefits —all while maintaining a consistency of message. (See Chapter Three for techniques in coaching your emerging leaders accordingly.) Some key questions to address are:

➤ What is to be achieved, how, and why?

➤ What will that outcome look like?

➤ What specific results are you seeking and why?

➤ What role will you play in the change?

➤ What role will be played by those you are asking to engage in the change?

➤ How will those changes affect everyone involved?

During these dialogues, remember to promote and encourage good listening skills. Answer questions and remove the ambiguity associated with change initiatives. This approach leads to a feeling of empowerment that will more likely build enthusiasm and support for the project at hand.

Chapter Nine described the ways to teach emerging leaders how to develop flexible skills for leading a diverse workforce. If emerging leaders are to avoid the mistakes of their predecessors, they must know how to lead everyone involved in the execution of change. Remember, diversity goes beyond the traditional categories of gender, race, and ethnicity. Successfully guiding a diverse organization through a change initiative requires a repertoire of leadership techniques coupled with flexibility and an intuitive understanding of when each is most appropriate.

Emotional Intelligence is another critical component of flexibility. Leaders must know how to interpret and leverage emotions (theirs and others) in order to motivate and lead them in the desired direction. Good feedback and coaching skills (see Chapters One and Two) are, of course, essential in teaching one's direct reports how to be flexible when dealing with change. Good motivating and influencing skills (see Chapters Six and Seven) enhance one's flexibility, as does building relationships and managing conflict (see Chapters Four and Five). Conflict management skills are especially valuable in change initiative situations where competing interests and agendas exist within the organization. If these issues are not resolved at an early stage, key people may attempt to sabotage or divert the change process to suit their own narrow interests.

Sensitivity is a key component of flexibility. Leaders need to understand that everyone, from hourly employees to fellow executives, is threatened by change to one degree or another. Be compassionate and empathetic in understanding the fears, confusion, or other challenges of anyone affected by a specific change. Listen honestly and be open to revising your plans. Find meaningful ways to engage in dialogue.

Remember, there is almost always a gap between the results a leader envisions and the best possible solution in the eyes of those whose problem is to be solved. But where there's a gap, there can be compromise. Learn to be flexible enough to find the happy medium. Where it's not possible to accommodate an individual or group, make sure they know their suggestions were taken seriously. Then use your influencing and motivating skills to create true followership despite reservations. Decades of change management initiatives (failures and successes) have shown people who feel a sense of ownership in change are much more likely to work toward its successful implementation. Leaders who possess and demonstrate empathy, compassion, and understanding in leading change, will garner support. When these are missing, people will always find a way, either passively or aggressively, to resist the change.

The ability to solicit cooperation is another essential type of flexibility that emerging leaders need to master change. "The primary task of management is to get people to work together in a systematic way," states Clayton M. Christensen, Matt Marx, and Howard H. Stevenson in "The Tools of Cooperation and Change" (*Harvard Business Review Online*, 2006). "It's a complicated job, and it becomes much more so when managers are trying to get people to change." The article lists a selection of tools for leaders contemplating change. They include:

> **Power Tools of Cooperation**—These include sanctions, force, coercion, and threats. These heavyweights are some times necessary to achieve agreement when the members of an organization are at loggerheads and consensus is tottering.

> **Management Tools**—Training, standard operating procedures, and measurement systems help focus teams on coordination and processes.

> **Leadership Tools**—These are results-oriented rather than process-oriented techniques. An example of a leadership tool is an energizing and inspiring vision statement that compels agreement about where the organization needs to go.

➤ **Culture Tools**—Rituals and folklore can foster a deep consensus on priorities. They also tweak a change-resistant culture to move it in the right direction.

The choice of tool is determined by two factors. First, the extent to which people agree on what they want (results, values, priorities, and trade-offs), and second, the extent to which they agree on what actions will lead to the desired outcomes. Have your coachees study the article by Christensen et al., for details and company case studies on the use of these tools. Then coach them to apply the correct tool depending on the situation. It will be an indispensable guide in helping them to develop flexibility—an essential leadership skill.

There is one final component of flexibility, and that, is execution. Sensitivity, communication, motivation, and influence create buy-in and move people into a position in which they are ready to cooperate, but something's missing. Without a clear execution plan, nothing will happen. If a change initiative can be likened to a long-distance race, execution represents the firing of the starting pistol. Before doing this, double-check that the technology or process chosen to guide your execution is a good fit for your culture. Don't assume that a system will work well for your organization simply because it's highly rated or was a resounding success in another organization. Maintain flexibility in examining the qualities, benefits, and liabilities of a variety of processes in collaboration with your team. Continually measure your progress. (Remember, what gets measured gets done.) Without measurement of success, people tend to lose confidence and momentum.

Adaptability and Resiliency

Emerging leaders often plow ahead with great enthusiasm, despite indications that things may not be going as expected. (In all fairness, this is also true of many leaders with decades of experience!) An antidote to this dangerous tendency is to adopt a scientific view of the entire change venture. Consider it an ongoing experiment in which trial and error are your teachers. In this regard, adaptability will be a crucial

Saboteurs At Work?

Are the people in your organization fed up with constant change-du-jour? If so, they are likely to sabotage any new change initiative. The word "sabotage" comes from the French sabot, which means "wooden shoe." A popular story has it that workers who were treated poorly in the early industrial age would throw their shoes in the machinery to make it grind to a halt. However, ask any machinist or mechanical engineer what a shoe is, and they'll describe it as a clamp holding a piece of metal in place. In the past, French railway workers on strike would cut the sabot that held railroad tracks in place.

In today's information age, of course, mechanical sabotage is relatively rare. But despite the many different forms it can take, sabotage is still sabotage. The relevant point here is this: When people in an organization are faced with unwanted or poorly executed change, whether on a machine shop floor or in a white-collar environment, they will find ways to thwart it. Savvy leaders know how to spot these problems in advance and how to defuse them.

leadership skill. It joins flexibility and execution as essential tools for both leaders and those in the trenches.

Adaptability is important for both leading and dealing with change. Adaptability means being able to roll with the punches, adjust to uncertainties and new challenges, integrate new knowledge and apply it to ever-changing circumstances. The very nature of change implies that nothing is cast in stone. Even the best-tested formulas provided by change management gurus are merely intelligent options and not universal truths. So, if a formula does not appear to fit at any point during execution, an adaptable leader stops the bus, backs up, pulls out the roadmap, and finds ways to detour or chart a new course. Of course, the sooner a leader becomes aware of a barrier to execution, the better.

Remember to coach your emerging leaders to solicit feedback across multiple levels, use good listening skills, and stay attuned to the needs, fears, and concerns of everyone around them.

A trait closely allied with adaptability is resiliency. "When change takes place, it is not the strongest or most intelligent individual who survives," wrote Al Siebert, director of *The Resiliency Center and author of The Resiliency Advantage: Master Change, Thrive Under Pressure, and Bounce Back From Setbacks* (Berrett-Koehler Publishers, 2005) in the ASTD article "Develop Resiliency Skills" (Training & Development, September 2006). "Survivors are those who adapt and flourish in the new environment," says Siebert. Overly compliant individuals, trained to fit in and follow instructions, on the other hand, flounder in an environment of nonstop change. His resiliency model is built of these five levels that can be learned in the workplace:

1. Maintain good health and well-being as an antidote to workplace stress.

2. Demonstrate clear-headed and disciplined problem-solving abilities.

3. Possess self-confidence, healthy self-esteem, and a positive self-image.

4. Display optimism, self-confidence, self-motivation, and a contagious enthusiasm for learning.

5. Bounce back quickly from setbacks, generally emerging stronger than before.

When it comes to Level One Resiliency, good health and well-being are antidotes to workplace stress. Stress, in Siebert's view, is not a result of actual workplace conditions, but rather how people perceive what is happening around them. It's a mental and emotional interpretation of external events. Wellness programs and a corporate culture that support healthy lifestyles are powerful ways to combat what many experts call the "silent killer." Anxiety, anger, fear, and helplessness are less likely to accompany a change initiative in a positive workplace atmosphere.

Level Two Resiliency comes into play when people focus on clear-headed and disciplined problem-solving abilities. They face problems head-on and with gusto. This is a powerful and constructive alternative to disengagement, helplessness, and blaming others or becoming highly emotional. The more highly skilled problem solvers are able to shift from left-brain analytical thinking to right-brain creative thinking as required by the circumstances. To foster Level Two Resiliency skills, encourage your emerging leaders to develop high self-confidence by honing their problem-solving skills on various "what-if" scenarios.

Level Three Resiliency in Siebert's model deals with strong self-confidence, healthy self-esteem, and positive self-image. To develop these strengths, Siebert encourages emerging leaders to focus on their strengths rather than weaknesses and on what they have accomplished rather than their mistakes and failures.

Level Four Resiliency represents people who are optimistic, self-confident, self-motivated, and self-managed learners. These self-actualized individuals trust their intuitions, read others well, and calmly steer groups through chaos. "Leave highly resilient people alone to do what they believe is best," recommends Siebert. "Coach managers to listen to them and use them as in-house consultants."

Level Five Resiliency is demonstrated by those who bounce back quickly from setbacks, generally emerging stronger than before. They are the ideal (and most admired) leaders in a world of nonstop change. It's easy to see why. They flex, bend, and mend rapidly from disappointment. Even more surprisingly, they view challenging events as springboards and opportunities to experience greater levels of personal efficacy. To encourage the development of these strengths, coach emerging leaders to analyze why a problem occurred, what lessons can be learned from the negative experience, and how to get back on the horse.

Another important aspect of adaptability relates to a leader's response to the external environment. Adaptable leaders don't simply copy what competitors do or buy the latest enterprise software just because it's "hot." They adapt and help their teams adapt to new opportunities, threats, and changing customer expectations. They design carefully thought-out plans and use flexible strategies that leverage new knowledge and technology, but only if it fits and makes sense for the organization's culture and its stage of development.

How can you foster a spirit of adaptation in organizational culture? "The many difficulties involved in fostering adaptation in large organizations make it essential to have a culture with firmly embedded values and beliefs that support innovation and change," states Gary Yukl, author of *Leadership in Organizations* (Prentice Hall, 7th Ed., 2009)and Richard Lepsinger, coauthor of *The Art and Science of 360 Feedback* (Pfeiffer, 2nd Ed., 2009), in "Leading Change: Adapting and Innovating in an Uncertain World" (LIA, Vol. 26, No. 2, 2006). "Relevant values include flexibility, continuous improvement, initiative, and a quest for excellence. Instead of viewing adaptation as an infrequent reaction to dramatic, one-time events, it is better to view it as a continuous process that involves a combination of many and frequent incremental improvements and occasional major changes." Adaptable organizations nurture new ideas, employ flexible systems, and promote the free sharing of information. They encourage people to view problems from multiple perspectives, question old assumptions, and brainstorm better approaches.

Developing a High-trust Culture

People will always be people, and they will always question change. Whether a change is due to a reorganization, merger, or just the need for better ways of doing things, people will always wonder (silently or aloud), "What will it mean for me?" If this question is not answered fully to everyone's satisfaction, an environment of mistrust is born. That makes change exceedingly difficult. In The Enemies of Trust (*Harvard Business Review*, February 2003, Product No. R0302G), Robert Galford and Anne Seibold Drapeau discuss five factors that erode trust.

The first on the list is inconsistency in an organization's messages to employees, customers, shareholders, or other stakeholders. This includes every mistake from saying one thing and doing another, to the simplest, but most common sin of management, under-communicating or communicating inaccurately. People need clarity and accuracy. If you communicate a plan to them and that plan changes, people will be far more forgiving than if you simply don't articulate that plan at all or do so in anything less than an honest and transparent manner.

In addition to inconsistency in messaging, a related destroyer of trust is inconsistency in the application of standards. Favoritism, in any form, is a prime example. Misplaced benevolence also destroys trust. An example of this would be a well-meaning superior who overlooks incompetence or the disruptive behavior of "difficult" employees who refuse to work as a team.

Next up: "Elephants in the parlor." This trust-eroding factor occurs when leadership denies the existence of a politically charged situation. Employees are clearly aware that something is being concealed and they become suspicious. Finally, there's the elephant's first cousin, aptly titled, "rumors in a vacuum." This pattern arises when employees are given incomplete information about an initiative. In response, the company rumor-mill kicks into high gear and works overtime to "explain" the omission. While this scenario can be more entertaining than General Hospital, it's very destructive to an organization's esprit de corps.

Most organizations fall prey to the "enemies of trust" from time to time. We're all human, and it's just unrealistic to think mistrust can be avoided 100 percent of the time. Galford and Seibold Drapeau recommend a pragmatic, four-step approach to rebuilding trust when it has been violated: (1) Figure out what happened; (2) assess the damage; (3) own up to the loss quickly; and (4) identify needed remedial actions.

A "trust rebuilding" campaign represents a perfect time to coach emerging leaders on how to spot problems in advance as well as how to repair the damage after they occur. Observe your coachees in their interactions with peers, superiors, subordinates, customers, and other stakeholders, paying careful attention to any actions that create suspicion, rumors, and mistrust. That might include inconsistencies in messages or standards, holding back of important information, sugarcoating the truth, or other trust destroyers. Use candid feedback (see Chapter Two) to make them aware how others perceive their words and the adverse effects that can result. As always, set a good example by practicing what you preach.

A Pre-Flight and In-Flight Checklist for Change

➤ Gauge organizational readiness. Before launching any change initiative, carefully consider these three questions: Do we need to change? How will we execute it? How will we measure its effectiveness?

➤ Don't dictate change from above. Tap into people's passions to get them excited about it. Paint an alluring picture of the future and everyone's role in it.

➤ Study past successes and failures and remain open to learning along the way. Case histories of change initiatives are an excellent source of material.

➤ Be fully accountable for the process. You're a leader. Do your job. Don't leave a change initiative up to a project team. Just like in the military, the troops look to their leaders (executive team) for direction. They want to be assured (emotionally and intellectually) that change is possible and the right thing to do.

➤ Walk the talk in your actions and attitude. Remain optimistic and confident that the change will succeed and result in the desired outcome.

➤ Don't be afraid of losing control. Loosen your grip on the reins and learn to trust the process and your people. "An organization coming unfrozen under an overload of experimentation and new ideas is a terrifying thing for traditional leaders," states Richard Tanner Pascale, Mark Millemann, and Linda Gioja in "Changing the Way We Change" (*Harvard Business Review*, 1997). "Matters seem out of control, which to a degree they are. But as leaders weather this storm, they begin to undergo a shift in mindset. From thinking, 'I've got to stay in control' or 'This is too fast,' they develop an ability to operate outside their comfort zone and accept ambiguity and adversity as a part of the design." Keep the faith. If you've laid the groundwork properly, things will turn out well.

➤ Don't underestimate the psychological foundations of change adversity. They require study and understanding. Learn to recognize and overcome them in yourself and others through conversations and awareness.

➤ Remove organizational barriers to change. These include silos, cultural norms from a bygone era (e.g., "we've always done it that way"), sacred cows, and outdated technology.

➤ Coach a group of emerging leaders to execute a change initiative together. Recently, a large Western power utility piloted an ongoing "change leadership council" of emerging talent from five key departments. These executives are receiving tremendous developmental benefits as individuals, as well as learning to cooperate and collaborate for the greater good of the organization.

➤ Consider retaining the services of a change management consultant. While this decision can lighten the load for a leader, it only works if the change management consultant is fully integrated into the organizational culture as a trusted advisor and possesses the components of flexibility and adaptability outlined in this chapter.

➤ Implement change initiatives in small bites. Even in the largest and most comprehensive organizational "makeovers," initiatives can be broken down into manageable components. Stress the importance of viewing the process as a multi-course gourmet meal as opposed to forcing the proverbial pig through the python. Challenge your organization to have fun with the initiative. Humor and light-heartedness can make any task—even arduous ones—easier, less stressful, and more successful in the long run.

Change Is the Only Constant

Change never stops. It occurs every day, even when nothing seems to be happening on the surface. That's why flexibility and adaptability are absolute essentials in an executive's leadership toolkit.

Before hiring or promoting individuals to leadership roles, make sure your selected candidates have the ability to deal strategically with change. Begin this process by asking your HR or OD department to administer a battery of assessments to potential leaders to determine if they have what it takes to succeed. If the foundation is there, build your coaching program around developing existing strengths, using the assessment results to guide your efforts. However, don't try to teach what you don't already know and never practice on a daily basis. You will be perceived as a phony, and your efforts will be doomed to failure. Be direct, clear, and honest and walk the talk. It's the best way to help your coachees avoid the mistakes of their predecessors and get a jump-start in their new roles as organizational leaders.

A Tool for Soliciting Feedback

An excellent tool for soliciting feedback is the Work Environment Survey (WES). These questionnaires anonymously and frequently poll large numbers of people involved in change, affected by it, or watching it rush in their direction like a tidal wave. The surveys assess the reaction of all these constituents and provide critical data that can help improve the outcome of a change initiative. The WES can be scaled to meet the needs of very small organizations, and work equally well for companies with hundreds, even thousands of people. Using the WES is an excellent way to accurately assess how clearly a leadership team is communicating its message, how well the change plan is being executed, and the degree to which the organization is succeeding or failing in its overall efforts to strategically manage change.

Additional Resources

Flexible Leadership: Creating Value by Balancing Multiple Challenges and Choices by Gary Yukl and Richard Lepsinger, Pfeiffer, 2004.

"Leading Change: Adapting and Innovating in an Uncertain World" by Gary Yukl and Richard Lepsinger, *LIA*, Vol. 26, No. 2, May/June 2006, pp. 3–7.

"Changing the Way We Change" by Richard Tanner Pascale, Mark Millemann, and Linda Gioja, *Harvard Business Review*, www.harvardbusiness.org, Product No. 97609, 1997.

"Intentional Change" by Richard Boyatzis and Annie McKee, *Journal of Organizational Excellence*, Summer 2006, pp. 49–60. Published online by Wiley InterScience, www.interscience.wiley.com.

"The Tools of Cooperation and Change", by Clayton M. Christensen, Matt Marx and Howard H. Stevenson. *Harvard Business Review*, www.harvardbusiness.org, Product No. R0610D, 2006.

"Develop Resiliency Skills: How valuable life lessons can breed resiliency" by Al Siebert, Ph.D., www.astd.org, September 2006.

The Resiliency Advantage: Master Change, Thrive Under Pressure, and Bounce Back from Setbacks by Al Siebert, Ph.D., Berrett-Koehler Publishers, 2005.

"The Real Reason People Won't Change" by Robert Kegan and Lisa Laskow Lahey, *Harvard Business Review*, www.harvardbusiness.org, Product No. R011OE, 2001.

Leading Change by John P. Kotter, Harvard Business Press, 1996.

The Heart of Change: Real-Life Stories of How People Change Their Organizations by John P. Kotter and Dan S. Cohen, Harvard Business Press, 2002.

"The Enemies of Trust" by Robert Galford and Anne Seibold Drapeau, *Harvard Business Review*, www.harvardbusiness.org, Product No. R0302G, 2003.

CHAPTER ELEVEN

HOW TO IDENTIFY COMPETENT TALENT—A CHECKLIST FOR LEADERS

Of the best leader, when he is gone, they will say: We did it ourselves.
— Chinese Proverb

Grooming a new generation of leaders is a challenge that's as old as leadership itself. While it may seem like an absolutely overwhelming task, it doesn't have to be. In fact, the necessary steps often fall into place quite naturally once the first hurdle—the process of identifying the right talent for development—is overcome. Since developing talent is a crucial task, and one that most organizations don't practice very well (if at all), we're going to dedicate an entire chapter to it. If you and your organization are not already well on the road to identifying and developing talent, you're almost too late. But, there is still time to start and that time is now!

Caution: Leadership Vacuum Ahead

There is no doubt about it: the retirement bubble will burst soon, creating a leadership vacuum like none before in history. For organizations that have not prepared a new generation of executives to fill the void, a potential crisis of disastrous proportions looms just over the horizon.

The first wave of Baby Boomers (people born between 1946 and 1964) began turning sixty on January 1, 2006—a trend initially expected to continue at a rate of eight thousand a day until 2024. In 2008–09, the economic crisis forced some people to postpone their retirement plans as they saw their 401Ks turn into "201Ks." This has given their employers a short reprieve, but only a year or two, at the most. Once the economy picks up and portfolios begin to recover, the exodus and brain drain of Baby Boomer executives will resume—and, very likely, at a breakneck pace.

When it comes to identifying potential leadership talent, veteran leaders need to be honest, direct, objective, and pragmatic. Organizations waste far too much time on the politics and political correctness of promotions rather than developing and promoting the right people for the right jobs. Leadership is about "doing the right thing," as opposed to management, which focuses on "doing things right." It's important for leaders to take charge without the fear of bruising a few egos and choose instead to promote the best person even though he or she may be less popular than other potential candidates. The fact is: when people are promoted for the right reasons, they tend to work twice as hard as those who advance in their careers simply by warming the right chairs and not making any egregious mistakes. Individuals who were passed over for promotion will make it their business to find out why. If they are leadership material, they will fill in the gaps in their skill set and try, try again until they succeed.

In this chapter you will learn how to identify competent emerging talent. But be forewarned: this is not a journey for the faint-hearted. It may require you to go against the grain of what is commonly ac-

Special Tip

Many executives wrongly assume that succession planning is the HR department's job. Nothing could be further from the truth! Leadership development—whether in a business unit or the entire organization—falls squarely on the shoulders of the current leaders. An organization's leaders have a responsibility to plan for succession and to create bench strength for the future. An organization's current leaders are in the best position to identify and groom their successors. HR should be a resource in the process, but in a supportive manner, not an executive capacity. The vision, planning, and execution of an effective succession management initiative must come from the leaders who will be stepping aside one day and welcoming the new generation of executives on board.

cepted as organizational wisdom. You will also likely push against the processes and "logic" of HR and how it views success. Their goal, and process, is to get "names in a box" and call it a day. Actual identification and development is typically not their forte. No one, and I mean no one, is in a better position to identify and develop future leaders than you! This chapter is for leaders, not managers or others outside of your

Promoting—Wrong and Right

As a director in the communications industry, "Tom" had successfully completed a number of tough assignments and was promoted to VP to manage the largest undertaking of change management in the corporation's history. His superb presentations indicated stellar results throughout his organization. However, an objective analysis (including interviews with peers) would have revealed a very different picture: It turns out that Tom was a very poor project and people manager, avoided conflict, and steered clear of risks. About ninety days after Tom's promotion, his superiors began to see that in areas requiring very strong skills, Tom was, in fact, quite weak. His inability to manage people and projects was costing the company millions.

On the other hand, "Georgina" was a well-educated and highly capable junior executive in the legal department of a large corporation. She possessed great potential and sincerely wanted to broaden her skill set and advance in her career. The leader of another business unit became aware of Georgina, and he quickly hired her. Considerable time, effort, and resources were spent in creating opportunities for her. Georgina was actively supported, coached, and mentored. Part of that process involved gradually giving her broader responsibilities. Within a year, she advanced from running a small department of three direct reports to leading over thirty people.

The story doesn't end there. Georgina continued to advance, redesigning her new organization so that it ran with greater efficiency. Not surprisingly, her work came to the attention of yet another business unit, which successfully recruited her. Once again, Georgina found herself in an entirely different area of the business—a far step from her law background—and once again doubled the number of her direct reports. Again, with the appropriate resources, support, and coaching, she excelled and is now under consideration for a new role in yet another business unit. Each career move for Georgina involved leaving her comfort zone, but she did so successfully, due in part to her superiors' good sense in planning her development coupled with her own courage, "can-do" attitude, and impressive abilities.

sphere of expertise, influence, or control! It's about doing the things that are best for your organization rather than simply doing things the right way. The goal is for you to learn how to orchestrate a process of thoughtful and pragmatic succession planning to create bench strength and a leadership legacy for your organization.

What You See Is What You Get... Or Is It?

Talent comes in many flavors. The temptation is to choose the most obvious—young barnstormers who crave adulation, adore the spotlight, and constantly make sure that everyone knows what a great job they are doing. These stars manage up effectively. Their great executive presence and superb presentation skills make them winners of organizational "beauty contests." They dazzle so brightly they often leave senior leaders blind to their potential weaknesses. In fact, one of the most common flaws of these divas is a tendency not to give proper credit to the subordinates whose work was instrumental in their success. Those tiny flaws begin to loom larger after these corporate celebrities are promoted. Fatal cracks begin to appear in their beautiful veneer, and the Peter Principle ("In a hierarchy, employees tend to rise to their own level of incompetence.") becomes glaringly obvious. To make matters worse, the promotion usually creates dissatisfaction among former peers who contributed to the star's success and were, in fact equally, if not more, deserving of advancement.

In some cases, however, shining stars may actually be genuine executive material. Their strong charisma may coexist with a terrific work ethic, real business savvy, and legitimate project successes; in other words, they may be tremendous potential leaders. How can you spot the difference between them and their empty-suit counterparts? Step 3 below will show you how to make the distinction. Then you can avoid the all-too-human temptation to overlook potentially superb candidates and begin moving them out from behind the deep shadows cast by the organization's brightest stars.

Watch for the Unsung Heroes

It's now time to praise the most chronically overlooked talent in an organization: those unassuming yet ultra-competent managers who avoid fanfare and the limelight. These are the low-key, hard-working individuals who know how to marshal resources, get jobs done on time and within budget. Unlike their puffed-up counterparts, they conscientiously and humbly give credit where credit is due. No doubt you're familiar with the type. Like most of us, you probably benefit from their efforts each day!

These unsung heroes of an organization are most typically found in support positions behind VPs, team leaders, and project leaders. They quietly work behind the scenes to make their superiors successful. They establish excellent working relationships and networks, and possess the trust and credibility of everyone around them. But because they don't toot their own horns, they're easily overlooked and taken for granted. Many of them eventually leave for better opportunities.

Of course, not all unsung heroes represent leadership potential. There are those who prefer to fly below the radar because they don't want to be challenged or stretched. While they may perform well at their current level, they just don't have the interest or capability to move up. These are not the people you want to develop for your leadership pool.

Most leaders are not objective enough to apply the scrutiny necessary to distinguish between these different flavors of talent. That's why it's necessary to have processes in place—including assessments—that present a complete, unbiased picture.

Build a Talent Pool

Recently, a biotech company faced a severe succession crisis. With little advance notice, their VP of human resources left. The problem was that in his four years on the job, the VP had not developed good bench strength below him. As a result, no internal candidate was prepared to immediately replace him. The company went into full scramble mode and began an expensive, time-consuming nationwide search. The company knew that even if the best possible candidate had been identified the next day or the next week, that individual would need to provide thirty to sixty days' notice to his or her current employer before leaving. To make matters worse, the biotech company, by selecting a relatively unknown person from outside the organization, would be taking a substantial risk.

When an outsider was ultimately chosen—a highly capable HR executive from a noncompeting industry—he faced two struggles starting on day one: the realization that the entire HR organization was the guiltiest party company-wide of having weak succession and no bench strength; and next, that he would now have to spend an inordinate amount of time "learning the ropes" of the company, its culture, and most importantly, who his own players were.

Needless to say there were "lines at his door" of people in his department "kissing up" and attempting to get in good with the new boss. Fortunately for him, and unfortunately for them, he was savvy to this game and took it all with a grain of salt. He took the time to make his own assessment based on observation and interviews with his peers about his department's staff and their actual effectiveness.

Six months later when it came time for him to lay out the department's new org chart, many were surprised about his choices for succession; they were not what "conventional wisdom" seemed to dictate. His choices were based on fact, not conjecture, obligation, or external pressure. Rather, they were based on assessment, performance, and potential—all real indicators of talent.

Finding and grooming a proven performer from the inside is almost always a safer and more efficient option. The problem is that few companies know how to initiate a valid internal search process that goes beyond the "beauty contest" model so often employed. The typical internal search generally amounts to hastily promoting the nearest shining star in the organization. The results tend to be predictable and disappointing, but there is a better way. Here is a common-sense, four-step succession planning process that any organization can follow:

Step 1: Open the communication channels across multiple levels.

Schedule an off-site meeting with executives and managers at several levels. Ask each participant to prepare for the meeting by making a list of the following:

➢ People who could conceivably succeed them

➢ People who could succeed those successors

➢ People who might succeed the second group of successors

Most participants will find it extremely difficult to think of even a handful of people per group for the simple reason that succession planning is a topic they've never considered seriously.

Step 2: Develop lists of successors and match names to positions.

At the off-site meeting, develop a list of positions and tentatively assign names of successors for one, three, and five years into the future. Begin with obvious talent—the shining stars—but only those who have proven themselves worthy of advancement. Then, list the potential hidden talent, including the unsung heroes.

Step 3: Assess talent.

Following the meeting, objectively assess the talent in line for future leadership positions. Traditional performance reviews can serve as a preliminary assessment tool, but true objectivity requires a level playing field, the kind provided only by impartial assessment instruments. Consider using personality assessment tools like the Harrison InnerView (www.harrison-innerview.com) or 360 Degree Feedback surveys (see the Appendix). Evaluate the individual's entire repertoire—not just technical abilities—and pay special attention to the qualities of leadership and people skills. Take a good, hard look at actual results. How consistent are the high scores of the organization's stars? How many projects did they actually complete? How many tough assignments have they tackled successfully? Was the success sustainable? Was achievement largely due to loyal, hard-working subordinates? Were they given credit? Who among the organization's pool of hidden talent possesses true leadership potential and who should remain in their current support positions? Beware of dazzling "fair-haired children" and the backstage parents who champion their cause!

Step 4: Create a strategic development plan.

After assessing each candidate's strengths, weaknesses, competencies, and capabilities, create a customized, personalized plan to develop each individual for the intended future position. This may include formal education, training, coaching, and mentoring, as well as stretch assignments and test roles. Remember, this process is not just "names in boxes"—it has to have teeth, a plan with timelines, and the expectation that it will be executed, not just talked about. Development is based in the reality of helping people get their hands dirty. The best way to accomplish that is to stretch them through actual assignments. It's the only way they will grow!

This simple, but comprehensive succession planning process provides a foundation upon which to build bench strength in the organization. It serves as a template for ongoing objective analysis and pragmatic decisions regarding how the organization hires and promotes people.

If followed, it will add value to the organization, promote growth, and create potential for greater success.

Above all else, don't procrastinate. Get started on succession planning "yesterday." Make it one of the top five initiatives of your organization's strategic plan for this quarter, not "this year." Business is not just about markets and financials; it's primarily about people. And the optimal way to attract, hire, retain, and promote the best people for an organization is by implementing a strategic succession planning process. This is how the top companies in the world identify and develop potential talent, and how they ensure a smooth transition from one organizational "generation" to another.

Lead Courageously

Taking a direct and honest approach to succession planning is very uncomfortable for leaders who hate disappointing people (conflict averse) or who are afraid of taking chances (risk averse). But the fact is: a leader's job is to actively advance the interests of the entire organization, not to tiptoe around people's feelings. Sometimes the job requires disappointing shining stars or antagonizing colleagues who have big plans for their favorite stars. But let's be real: This isn't junior high school. It's the business world and we're all adults. If people are so thin-skinned that they can't rise above occasional disappointment, learn from it, and improve their game, do they really belong in leadership positions in your organization to begin with?

Risk-averse people-pleasers rarely make effective leaders. They tend to promote people for all the wrong reasons, and the result is pain and suffering for their organizations. My coaching advice is always the same: don't worry about the individual; do what's right for the organization.

A large corporation in the entertainment industry was recently on the receiving end of that "tough-love" advice. "Harold," a long-time employee, was expecting a promotion. However, he was such a poor performer that he should have been fired. Coaching was suggested for Harold, but he refused (apparently, he had more important things to do!) The company was concerned about its potential liability should they dismiss him, and they were afraid that other employees would leave if he were fired.

For nearly three months, Harold's boss was coached on the importance of documenting Harold's poor performance. As he began to compile the data, he realized just how detrimental Harold's deficien-

Advice for Emerging Leaders

Remember the classic tale of the tortoise and the hare? Slow and steady wins the race. At least in terms of succession planning and developing the careers of potential leaders, there is great truth in this tale. Rushing emerging talent up the ladder too quickly may end in a precipitous fall from the top. A long-term, strategic approach to career development, even if it's slower in the short term, is a better way to sustainable success. Here's an example:

"Brad" was a director in the automotive industry whose excellent performance and great people management skills attracted the attention of senior leaders. When he was approached for a well-deserved promotion, Brad declined. He stated that he was not ready for a VP role and that he believed he could add far more value in his current position if senior leadership were to broaden the scope of his current responsibilities. Excuse me? Strange but very true!

A plan was developed to increase Brad's responsibilities incrementally while paying him executive compensation until he was truly ready to be VP. His realistic assessment of his strengths and developmental opportunities is rare, but along with proactive planning in cooperation with his superiors, laid a solid foundation that will ensure his future growth and success. Today, he sits in an SVP role and is "well-rounded." "Ready" is an understatement.

cies were. The boss finally summoned the courage to take an unpopular stand and fire him. No litigation ensued and, although a few of Harold's protégées left with him, the remaining team became stronger than ever. Harold had been the weakest link, and everyone had accommodated him. Once he was gone, the company raised its performance standards, and productivity went through the roof.

We hear so much rhetoric today about courageous leadership. What is it? True courage manifests itself in the ability to make the right decision even when it defies popular opinion, conventional wisdom, political correctness, or "we've-always-done-it-that-way" cultural norms. To achieve the greater good for the organization, leaders need to step up and speak with candor and honesty. As risky and discomforting as this can be, remember this: When you speak the truth, you're rarely the only one in the room thinking it. You're merely the one who has the courage to say it aloud. Take the risk, and in the end, the benefit will be well worth it.

The Leadership Imperative

What keeps executives from developing the next generation of leaders? Sometimes the omission has an emotional foundation. Let's face it: contemplating the need to groom a successor means confronting one's own corporate mortality. It can feel a bit like making a will. Try not to think of it as the beginning of demise, but rather as an opportunity to create a legacy—the legacy of success passed down to the next generation of leadership—by you!

Making wise choices in developing and promoting strong players is not just about retirement. It also has immediate benefits. The most obvious one first: it will make your job a lot easier! Think about it: greater bench strength will give you the opportunity to delegate more efficiently and effectively to capable, responsible people who need stretch and growth opportunities. Second, your organization will attract higher-caliber candidates from outside the company or from other business units. The clear, positive message that promotion is based on hard work and motivation—not on the management of superiors' perceptions—will attract desirable people and deter those with other agendas.

As Baby Boomers leave the workforce in growing numbers, the intellectual capital of organizations will depart with them unless it can be transferred to the next generation. In most companies, emerging leaders are not yet ready to take over. That's why it's crucial for current leaders to begin to prepare them. While it's not possible to stem the tide of exiting retirees, immediate action can at least stop the brain drain. If you are among those soon to retire, your leadership position comes with the obligation to develop emerging talent. Welcome to one of the most deeply rewarding (and enjoyable) activities of your career!

Special Tip

Be sure to plan enough time to develop a candidate for a currently vacant or near-term future position. Few people realize what a lengthy process that can be. Depending on the position and the industry, it may require years! In an ideal world, an internal candidate could fill every open position in an organization, but that's not always possible or practical. Start a search for outside talent as soon as you're aware of a potential, future vacancy. It's the best way to ensure a new employee can be properly groomed and critical positions won't be left unfilled for months on end. This is particularly important in highly technical industries such as pharmaceuticals, biotech, and engineering, where the talent pool is comparatively small and potential executives are in high demand. Finding and developing technically astute individuals who are also effective leaders of other people is an intensely time-consuming process. Don't wait until the retirement bubble bursts to begin your search. And remember, a tech-savvy person does not a good leader make—the people side of leadership is where most newly promoted leaders die on the vine. These are skills that if not a dominant aspect of someone's make-up requires time to develop.

Additional Resources

For additional resources and tips visit our website at
www.checklistforleaders.com

APPENDIX
ASSESSMENTS
SETTING THE STAGE FOR
DEVELOPMENT

The real voyage of discovery is not in seeking new landscapes, but in having new eyes.

— Marcel Prous

Before launching a development program of any kind for your emerging leaders, it is essential to assess their strengths and weaknesses. Since most of us have blind spots about ourselves, we cannot give an unbiased and fully accurate appraisal of our own strengths and weaknesses, nor can we serve as the only source of an objective evaluation of those around us. Accordingly, it's important to use a process to gather performance data in an objective and dispassionate way. The best place to start assessing emerging leaders is by using a 360-degree feedback instrument. A 360-degree assessment is essentially a behavioral and performance-related snapshot in time. The qualities it measures are subject to change, as opposed to an individual's innate personality traits, which remain fairly stable over time. It gathers feedback concerning the emerging leader from people all across the organization who have contact with that individual – superiors, peers, colleagues and direct and indirect reports.

There are other tools that complement a 360-degree instrument and can further the assessment and development of current and future leaders. The most common are the Myers-Briggs Type Indicator (or MBTI, which is administered to about two million people a year), the DiSC Personal Profile System and Harrison InnerView, to name a few. (Please refer to the resources listed at the end of this chapter for more information on these tools.) Additionally, a number of Emotional Intelligence measurements, although newer to the marketplace, have been embraced by organizations and possess a high level of credibility even in these early stages of use.

In terms of administering assessments, at the more extreme end of this spectrum are those organizations with formal assessment centers of their own. In these centers, individuals perform specific drills and maneuvers (staged by actors, usually) to assess employee skills in a range of real-time scenarios. Participants are presented with crisis and non-crisis situations, and the plans and strategies they develop in response to them are observed and measured. The program ends with an assessment report that serves as a basis for coaching and related personal and professional development activities. These assessment summaries also play into future promotion and succession models.

Select the Right 360-degree Instrument

The first challenge is to select the appropriate 360-degree instrument from the wide range of off-the-shelf tools available in the marketplace. In this regard, it's important to maintain a "buyer-beware" attitude. Conduct research to find the right tool for your organization and your people. Chances are, your own HR department will have one in place or be able to recommend a high-quality choice. The assessment should accurately measure the core competencies identified by company leadership as critical for emerging leaders for your organization, along with specifically identifying developmental opportunities aligned with the company's goals. (Please refer to the sidebar in Chapter One for a list of sample core competencies.) In some cases, it is necessary to have the tool customized. Again, "buyer-beware" is the watchword. Some consulting firms provide this service at a reasonable price, while others charge upwards of $100,000 just to get you started.

Good 360-degree assessments and personality profiles are supported by an infrastructure of research and psychometric testing. Established vendors – which are not necessarily the biggest vendors – have accumulated enormous databases from assessments of hundreds of thousands, and in some cases, millions of people. Based on this data, normative averages have been established against which current and future leaders may be measured, taking into account their own demographic placement within an industry, a national and, in some cases, a worldwide frame of reference.

When evaluating the effectiveness of a 360-degree tool, another critical factor to consider is whether it asks the right questions when assessing the specific core competencies identified as essential for leaders in your organization. Broad questions that address generalized headings leave too much room for subjective interpretation and are therefore not as effective. Effective questions drill down into specific skills and behaviors to create a truly objective and in-depth view. For example, under the heading of an emerging leader's interpersonal skills, a good instrument asks questions to assess whether the individual:

➤ Communicates effectively with others

➤ Demonstrates sensitivity towards the feelings and needs of others (is empathetic and a good listener, for example)

➤ Is proactive in building meaningful relationships across his or her own area and throughout the organization

➤ Engenders an atmosphere of trust with co-workers

➤ Deals with conflict in a solutions-oriented way that produces outcomes beneficial to all concerned.

Let's now take a look at an entirely different skill development area. Under the heading of strategic management skills, a good instrument will determine if an individual:

➤ Adapts quickly and effectively to changing circumstances

➤ Correctly assesses the risks and returns of specific decisions

➤ Has a deep understanding of markets, competitors and customers

➤ Has a global perspective – if appropriate to your organization and its business focus

➤ Identifies and articulates a long-term vision for the future

➤ Properly manages relationships with third parties

➤ Understands strengths and weaknesses of the company.

If HR has already selected an assessment tool for your company, take the time to review the questions it asks. Make sure they are appropriate for the organization and its emerging leaders. If not, work with HR to focus the instrument as necessary. If your company has not yet chosen a tool, carefully investigate a number of instruments in cooperation with HR. Remember, if the assessment renders wrong or inadequate answers, your development program is doomed from the start!

Who Should Administer a 360-degree Assessment?

While HR professionals can help create a list of core competencies to be measured, and even point you towards an appropriate vendor, typically, they should not administer the assessment. Why? Although HR should serve a vital role in employee development, the department is often viewed as being "the police." As a result, both leaders and their protégés are often wary of the outcomes of an HR-controlled assessment and will not openly share the intelligence required to assess and coach your talent successfully.

To ensure openness, fairness and trust, a 360-degree assessment should be administered by an outside vendor or consulting company experienced in assessment, delivering feedback and executive coaching. Respondents to surveys administered by outside firms tend to be more honest and forthcoming in their opinions when their fears of punitive actions from HR – whether justified or not – are allayed. Moreover, and for the same reasons, assessed individuals are more inclined to speak candidly when instruments are administered by an objective outside consultant, particularly when it comes to discussing their identified challenges. An experienced consultant or external coach can also help assessed individuals as they compile an effective list of survey respondents – the key people who will provide the most accurate and well-rounded picture.

Administration of the 360-Degree Assessment

Assessed individuals should identify twelve to twenty-five potential respondents, representing all levels within the company. It is important for the list to include people with whom they have had contact frequently and recently – ideally, within the last six to twelve months. The next step is to anonymously survey these people, listing only their reporting relationship, not their names. Conduct such surveys online, if possible. Ask each respondent to rate the assessed individual on a scale of one to five on no less than fifty to seventy-five questions. Those questions should cover all the essential competencies identified by the employer for anyone who manages people in the company. Eight to twelve competency categories are average, although some organizations use even more in their assessments.

Evaluate every aspect of the individual's performance and behavior. Be sure to ask superiors of the assessed individual to rank the level of importance of skill in each competency for the individual's position. At a minimum, the emerging leader's boss, peers and direct reports should be surveyed. Sometimes the list includes external stakeholders or a peer group outside the individual's functional area. Make sure three or more people provide feedback in each category and that they are people who can be counted on for honest and direct feedback – not best friends or worst enemies! Trends in behavior and performance will emerge whether the respondent's list is slanted or not. Ideally, the list should be well-rounded and contain a potentially wide range of respondents.

After collecting the data, it should be averaged and compiled. Next, develop and deliver a narrative report to the coachee by a coach. The report may synthesize the 360-degree data with results from other types of assessments for a full picture. The precise format of the report depends on the company's priorities, but should include important sections such as the following:

➤ Top leadership strengths

➤ Impact of personality style on leadership skills

➤ Potential challenges

➤ Development areas

The last of these is usually ranked according to the level of skill and its importance in the boss's judgment. For example, if an individual ranks low in a skill that is considered extremely important in the organization, it becomes a primary component in the coachee's development plan. If the coachee ranks high in a skill that is considered of great importance, that strength can be leveraged in coaching to help raise skill levels in other areas. If the coachee ranks low in a skill that is of low importance to the boss, its development can wait.

Too often, 360-degree results are improperly administered and the results incorrectly delivered. In such unfortunate cases, what ranks highest is considered a strength, and what ranks lowest becomes a development area. This may actually create an inaccurate overall picture. Without diligently considering the "importance factor" at both ends of the scale, the data is of little value. In fact, it may misdirect a leadership candidate's development. Worse still, it can potentially lead the individual down a grievously wrong path – for example, believing in and acting upon the "wrong strengths."

After coachees have reviewed their reports, they should meet with their coaches (or their boss-as-coach, as the case may be) to discuss the findings. Walking through the entire report together, they make some preliminary decisions concerning developmental focus areas. If a coach is not a coachee's boss, a second meeting should be scheduled in which the coachee can walk the boss through the report. At the end of this meeting, coach, boss and coachee meet in order to reach a consensus on the primary focus areas of the individual's development. And then the real work begins!

In many cases, the results of an assessment mark a turning point for coachees. Building an awareness of developmental needs is the first step toward change. Some may already have been highly motivated to improve, but had no idea how they were perceived by people around them. With others, it may take a couple of coaching sessions to move past defensiveness to acceptance and finally to motivation. This can even be true for your "best people." It is not uncommon for high performers to resist negative feedback – even if it is constructive – for fear it may "tarnish" their already stellar record. Let's face it – we're all human!

The coachee may also believe others are wrong in their assessments. However, since 360-degree tools measure perceptions of skills rather than actual skills, the perceptions of others are their reality, regardless of what the coachee thinks. The goal here is to manage the perception of others. Don't skip the steps of awareness, acceptance and motivation! Until the coachee is truly motivated to change, coaching will not be successful.

Finally, create a meaningful development plan that will result in a positive, constructive and productive experience for the emerging leader. Have the coachee work on no more than two competencies in a six- to nine-month period, beginning with those that are of the highest importance and in which the individual ranks lowest.

Mistakes to Avoid

Unfortunately, data gleaned from 360-degree assessments are sometimes grossly misused. Here are a few caveats:

➢ Never allow broad access to the coachee's 360-degree data. Reserve the raw data for the person being assessed. Neither HR nor the individual's coach or superior should be able to see the entire report. Only summaries of data collected should be released, such as the top ten strengths, top ten weaknesses and top five areas that have the greatest impact on an assessed individual's function.

➢ Never use 360-degree feedback data for a witch-hunt or as a way to assess a problem individual in preparation for punitive action or firing. Doing so even once will surely "poison the pot" and make others extremely reluctant to engage in future 360-style processes.

➢ Never distrust negative data on your favorite rising star. In your eyes, the individual may be the top performer who can do no wrong, regardless of everyone else's feedback. Everyone shows different faces to different people. Once a developmental opportunity or trend has consistently emerged from the assessment, never veto or override the feedback to protect an emerging leader from the scrutiny of others.

➤ Never assess others without going through your own 360-degree assessment. Sometimes, the greatest temptation of leaders is to bring in consultants to assess and "fix" the people around them, but refuse to be assessed themselves. Leaders who are not willing to participate in the process will operate from their own blind spots. They can neither effectively support professional growth in others nor reach a higher level of success for themselves. They and the people for whom they serve as role models will continue to operate in their comfort zones, not from a place of stretch, risk and potential growth.

Accentuate the Positive

In our busy work lives, few of us have the opportunity to stop running long enough to take a good look at ourselves and consider our strengths and weaknesses. Assessments, whether based on data from others (as in a 360-degree instrument) or on self-assessment questionnaires (such as MBTI and Emotional Intelligence), should be viewed as gifts. They provide an excellent opportunity to take an honest and potentially invaluable snapshot of ourselves at a specific point in our lives and careers. They help us better understand our own personalities, behaviors, strengths and the value we bring to our work environment. At the same time, they clarify our weaknesses and our opportunities for development.

Too often, the temptation – even for a conscientious coachee – is to fixate on the negative, despite the fact that it typically amounts to only a tiny percentage of the assessment results. Avoid this at all costs! Help your coachee avoid the pitfalls of feeling devastated, getting sidetracked or obsessively focusing on one or two weaknesses. Counsel them through these difficulties with understanding and encouragement. Perhaps share your own experiences as you went through similar "post-assessment blues."

In all effective assessments, the main concern is to focus on the strengths that have emerged, and to leverage them to turn weaknesses into opportunities for growth. The ultimate goal is for all of us to become better leaders and better people. Help your people see that their current strengths are like tools in their own "personal toolbox" – to be used to build a bright future!

Additional Resources

CPP, formerly Consulting Psychologists Press, publishes the Myers-Briggs Type Indicator tool and a variety of other assessment instruments; www.cpp.com, 800 624-1765.

For a variety of 360-degree instruments and other assessment tools, contact PPS International, www.ppsinternational.net, 800 606-5460, or Assessment Plus, www.assessmentplus.com, 800-536-1470, as a good start.

The Harrison InnerView tool for predicting, assessing and developing performance is published by Harrison InnerView, www.harrison-innerview.com.

For the DiSC assessment tool, contact Cornerstone Executive Development Group, www.cedg.com, 805 241-4200.

For information on Emotional Intelligence, contact TalentSmart, 11526 Sorrento Valley Road, Suite G, San Diego, CA 92191, (858) 509-0582, www.talentsmart.com.

Development Dimensions International, Inc., 1225 Washington Pike, Bridgeville, PA 15017-2838, (412) 257-0600, www.ddiworld.com.

Hay Group, The Wanamaker Building, 100 Penn Square East, Philadelphia, PA 19107-3388, (215) 861-2000, (215) 861-2111, www.haygroup.com.

.

17454201R00098

Made in the USA
Charleston, SC
12 February 2013